"When I Need Your Help, I'll Let You Know"

And Other Senior Myths That Can Lead to Disaster

Barbara Adler West, J.D.
and
Stephen F. Adler, Ph.D.

"When I Need Your Help, I'll Let You Know" And Other Senior Myths That Can Lead to Disaster, Copyright © 2017 by Barbara Adler West, J.D. and Stephen F. Adler, Ph.D.

All rights reserved. No part of this book may be used or reproduced in any manner whatsoever without written permission except in the case of brief quotations in critical articles or reviews.

The authors do not warrant that the information in this book is complete and up-to-date for every jurisdiction. The reader should not rely on the information in this book, and it is not intended to be a substitute for legal advice. If you have a specific question about a legal matter you should consult with an attorney in your state.

Published by Prominence Publishing.
www.prominencepublishing.com

Photography by Eliza Truitt.
www.elizatruitt.com

ISBN: 978-1-988925-51-6

First Edition: September 2017

Table of Contents

Foreword by Barbara Adler West, J.D. v

Foreword by Stephen F. Adler, Ph.D. xv

Straight Talk About Getting Old. xxiii

Myth #1: When I Need Your Help, I'll Let
You Know 1

    The Reality: You Won't Know When
You Need Help 8

    Tools for the Caregiver: Powers of
Attorney. 15

Myth #2: I Will Live In My Own Home Until
I Die. 19

    The Reality: You May Be Unsafe
at Home. 27

    Tools for the Caregiver: Thinking
Through Home-Based Care 28

Myth #3: When I Am Old, Ill and Dying,
My Family Will Take Care Of Me. 35

    The Reality: Family Members Aren't
Always Capable 42

    Tools for the Caregiver: Creating an
end-of-life Care Plan. 48

Myth #4: When I Can No Longer Manage My
         Money and Financial Affairs, A Trusted
         Person Will Handle My Finances..........55

   The Reality: Seniors Are Uniquely
   Vulnerable 62

   Tools for the Caregiver: What to do if
   a senior has been financially exploited.....66

Myth #5: I Don't Want To Do Any Estate
         Planning and I Don't Need A Will.
         When I Die, My Family Will Sort It Out....75

   The Reality: Creating a Will Or a
   Trust Is A Gift To Your Family 84

   Tools for the Caregiver: Capacity to
   make a Will or Trust...................88

Conclusion 91

In Memoriam 93

Glossary of Terms.............................95

Foreword by
Barbara Adler West, J.D.

In 1997, I hung out my shingle as an estate planning lawyer. More than half of the people who came through my door had questions about their parents that weren't always strictly legal. How do you provide help to a senior who needs help to stay independent and live safely at home but won't accept necessary services? How do you secure the property or financial accounts of a senior who is unaware that he is at risk of financial exploitation? How do you know when a court-established guardianship is the only answer to protecting another person and making sure that their needs are being met?

The issues that established me as an "elder law" attorney included guardianships, civil actions for restraining orders under the Vulnerable Adults Protection Act, and questions about the use and abuse of powers of attorney. There were also an astonishing number of consultations that centered on long-standing family tensions that had blossomed into the fulsome center of a family's need to take care of an ailing senior.

Ten years later, my family and I faced our own senior care crisis when my beautiful, talented, brilliant mother, Judy

Adler began to show signs of significant memory loss. I had always known that in 1939 my mom, her toddler brother and a cousin were subjected to radiation treatments for childhood ailments. Many years later, her doctors found she had developed a meningioma, a benign tumor, in her brain. Her doctors kept a watchful eye on her, taking scans for nearly a decade before they determined the tumor was growing. At the age of 74, she needed brain surgery.[1] After her brain surgery, post-operative complications and months of recovery, Mom underwent more radiation therapy to complete the destruction.

Those treatments seemed to sap her energy. For years we had lunch together on Saturdays after she and my dad went to Saturday Sabbath services at their synagogue. They'd been going to Temple together for 60 years, but she no longer cared to go with my father. Instead, he'd deliver her to my home and she'd nap on the living room couch with the cat. When I asked her why she didn't want to go to Temple anymore she told me that she had decided it was boring. I was shocked. "You've been an observant Jew and you've gone to Temple every week for 76 years," I challenged her. "Since when is it boring?," I asked. "76 years is enough," was all she would say.

She was never the same. The woman who always looked as though she had stepped out of a department store display window stopped caring about her weight and her

---

[1] The brain surgeon was optimistic, and he reminded us that although the tumor was benign, "there is no benign brain surgery."

clothes. An adult lifetime of Weight Watcher's diet plans went out the window. She began to skip dinner and move straight to dessert. With the loss of her food inhibitions, she put on pounds rendering useless her closets full of extra-small and petite-sized clothing. The inveterate shopper no longer cared if her sweater strained across her bust or if her slacks were out of season. She knew I was just trying to be nice, and she'd pretend mild interest when I brought her a new blouse or pair of slacks, but she would leave the new purchases, tags on, hanging over the back of a chair while she slid into the pants she had taken to wearing day after day. She dropped out of her creative writing class, gave up photography, and, after a while, she stopped reading. Even watching TV was difficult because she couldn't separate the commercials from the regular programming except if we watched a costume drama[2].

After a series of neurological tests, my mom was diagnosed with Alzheimer's disease and they showed us images of her brain where the tissue was dead. She couldn't remember whether she had eaten breakfast, but through the fog of her confusion and memory loss, she retained the memory of the neurologist who had diagnosed her with Alzheimer's. She never forgave the doctor or forgot her name. For the last 18 months of her life she refused to see any doctors at all. After

---

[2] We were deep into a British period drama when she turned to me and asked if I was enjoying the show. I assured her that I was. "Really?," she said. "Frankly these rich people and their problems are giving me a pain in the ***."

a while, she had to be reminded to shower and wash her hair. Eventually she forgot the tasks that followed showering and would sit wrapped in her towel until she was guided through the tasks of selecting socks, fastening her brassiere, choosing a clean top and slacks. She began to sleep more and more and stayed in her nightclothes all day. Eventually she slept 16 hours or more a day and ate only sporadically.

In September, we met with a social worker and talked about the changes in her sleeping and eating. Although we thought it would be my dad's choice, the doctor determined that she was now eligible for hospice care. I had the honor of being my mother's end-of-life care provider and was with her constantly for the last six weeks of her life. She was less and less oriented to time and place, but she knew me until the end. My dad had been taken ill and was hospitalized, so we were alone in their apartment. One night she wanted to walk and I helped her to and from her bed. She understood that my dad was ill and asked if I could spend the night with her. I told her yes and she smiled and held my arm a little a tighter, "Oh, Barby," she said, "You treat me like a queen. And I just love it." That was the last thing she said to me, and I was so happy that she knew until the end how much she meant to me.

My dad was in terrible pain awaiting a hip replacement and his mobility was limited, and then he fell ill with a bacterial infection and was hospitalized. My kids were out of town and I called them home. We drove straight from the airport to pick up our favorite take-out Chinese food. We were filling our plates in the dining room and laughing when I looked in on Mom and saw that she was gone.

There will never be anyone like her.

My mom died in her bed at home, never once admitting that she needed any help. Although her brain was slowly stopping its functioning, she was fortunate because her illness was virtually symptom-free. At the end of her life the blessing known as hospice care brought her the services and the medical services professionals who could keep her clean and comfortable and explain (finally!) what was happening to her. She was less feisty then, and enjoyed that help.

She was able to live and die as she wanted because she had the ongoing support of her husband, local family and the extended care community of outside caregivers. Not everyone is as lucky.

So why have we written this book? It began innocently enough as interesting conversation. Steve's professional background included corporate management. Over years of Sunday suppers, he listened as I talked about my more complex cases and the factors that seemed to make them so hard to resolve. During those years, personally and professionally, we acquired a range of perspectives on the subject of aging in America.

- *I have worked as an elder attorney for 25 years.* I have seen seniors living in squalor because this was their preference or because their caregivers were negligent, overwhelmed or had squandered financial resources that were supposed to last a lifetime; seen families splintered when one member commits financial exploitation of a senior relative; seen communities devastated when a senior dies from a long-term failure of proper care.

- *My Dad and Co-Author, Steve Adler, is a senior.* That's actually a pretty important credential because he's been walking the walk. He is actually the youngest 86 and one-half-year old man you will ever meet, with almost no grey hair.

- *We have been in-home caregivers.* Together, we provided months of in-home care to my mom after her brain surgery in 2009. We also hired and fired professional caregivers.

- *Steve was a caregiver for his wife.* He provided care to my mom until her Alzheimer's Disease made her completely dependent upon others to meet het daily care needs.

- *In his senior years, Steve has experienced his own health issues.* As Judy became more dependent, Steve was experiencing a trifecta of medical challenges. He wasn't mobile enough to provide care to her and needed help himself.

- *Steve and Judy brought paid caregivers into their home.* During their years living in congregate care, Steve and Judy had surgeries and hospital stays. On one occasion or another, in deference to the discharge plans, they brought professional services into the home. Knowing that the extra help was recommended, and, technically, a good idea, both Steve and Judy still chafed at the presence of an unfamiliar person in their private space. I remember Mom complaining that one caregiver smiled too much. Another, she said, never stopped talking. Steve found it unnerving when one caregiver ran the laundry for a single shirt or hand towel. She was just trying to be helpful, but it was clear that a live-in care provider would be more of a strain than a relief for my parents.

- *I took care of my Mom, and now I am helping take care of my dad.* About 2 months after my mom died, my dad underwent his hip replacement. The surgery was a breeze but he suffered post-operative complications that kept him in rehab for 4 months.

In thinking through the crises that envelop my senior clients and their families, we realized that there are two primary perspectives to the critical decisions we make as we age:[3]

1. **The senior** facing his own illness or the illness and mortality of a partner. This person may have

---

[3] While we're focusing our attention on these players, we acknowledge the importance of the senior's extended family and friends.

watched the decline or death of a long-term partner and is dealing with a myriad emotions, financial concerns and worry about what the future holds. The senior may be ill himself, depressed, anxious and unsure of how his disease will affect his ability to care for himself; the senior may be a caregiver who gets his own diagnosis of illness. With the death of a partner or upon a diagnosis, the senior may be suddenly faced with questions about moving. Moving is one of life's greatest stressors. The thought of moving after the loss of a loved one could be emotionally unbearable; the reality of the physical demands of packing alone could overwhelm a person who is grieving, ill or disabled. Fear of the unknown is not only paralyzing, it can color decision-making: What type and degree of disability looms ahead; what help will be needed over time and who will be there to assist; what help will cost and whether it will be tolerable or truly awful.

2. **The adult caregiver** who is trying to provide care or assistance to a senior. While watching the deteriorating senior, this person is also dealing with his own life. He may have his own health concerns, his day job, his marriage, money and relationship woes, sibling tensions and family disunity.

The seniors who have managed the transition from full independence to assisted living with the help of their families and friends are living the dream. These people have been able to develop a plan for the future and have implemented their strategy. Our focus is on the seniors who gave in to "wishful thinking" and made plans that were unsafe or unsustainable or that made them unwitting victims of fraud. Our goal is to identify for our readers the tall tales that seniors tell themselves and their families and explain why these are myths that can lead to unsafe, dangerous and even fatal outcomes.

* * * * *

This book is dedicated to the spirit of my dearest friend, Suzanne Keogh, who was lost to a rare and aggressive form of cancer in 2013. Suzanne was the funniest person I ever met and her sense of humor gave her the courage to look at life head-on, no matter how unappealing. She had worked finding in-home care and residential placements for seniors and she first wanted to write this book.[4] For years, we offered brown bag lunches to nursing aides and discharge planners looking for continuing education credit. We worked the library and senior-center circuit, scheduling public information meetings where we could talk about estate planning, pass out business cards, and

---

[4] When she was dying, I tried to be "in the moment" and talk about what might happen in her last days. "I'll get some of those smelly candles you like, and oils, and we'll have some New Age music playing," I proposed, trying to be open to the experience, whatever that meant. She was stern. "Barbara West," she said, (she called all her friends by their first and last names), "This is not going to be a spa date."

spark some new clients. These folks had come for the free donuts, but Suzanne wasn't going to let them doze.

"What do you think it will cost you live in an assisted community?" she'd bark.

"$4,000!" "$3,500!" "$2,200 a month!" The answers would be shouted back.

"WRONG!" Suzanne would thunder. Then she'd start talking about the state's average daily cost of skilled nursing care and why you shouldn't be fooled just because a place has fancy drapes in the lobby. Look at the state's nursing home safety reports. Ask how long the staff has been there. These are signs of a well-run community.

Suddenly I'd notice that no one was eating the donuts. "Get your heads out of the sand, people," Suzanne would insist, smiling but serious. Know your money, she'd say. Plan ahead. The cost of failing to plan is the loss of options and the highest possible expense.

The axiom, "Failing to plan is planning to fail," has been attributed to such luminaries as Winston Churchill and Benjamin Franklin, neither of whom had to plan for long-term care. Time Management guru Alan Lakein may have put it best: Planning is bringing the future into the present so you can do something about it now.

Or not. But don't say we didn't try to warn you.

Foreword by
Stephen F. Adler, Ph.D.

I was born in Berlin, Germany in 1930. My family had lived in Germany for centuries, and we are Jewish. We were swept up in the early stages of the racist madness that fueled World War II and became the Holocaust. In March 1939 I was sent to England on a ship along with other refugee children through a program called Kindertransport (Childrens' Transport). My father, mother and brother eventually made their way to safety in England, and in 1940 our family sailed to the U.S. and a new life in Chicago, where we had a sponsor.

Judy and I met in June of 1948. She was fifteen then and I was eighteen. We married n 1951 as I was working on my doctoral degree in chemistry. Judy had only completed a single semester of college. In 1954 we moved to Connecticut to follow my career. Our two daughters, Deborah and Barbara, were born there. We lived in a small ranch-style home at first, but by 1967 we had built a roomy four-bedroom home on an acre of tree-covered land. Judy stood guard as they cleared the land, defending her greensward. Our daughters completed public school education and both went on to the University of Connecticut. Even Judy went to college, at Bridgeport University, where she received a BS in Education although, having decided she didn't much like other people's children, she never taught so much as a single day of school.

I pursued a career as a research chemist and then moved into laboratory management. At the age of 50 I must say that I did not make plans for the future, nor did Judy push me to do so. Like so many people in our situation, we were enjoying being where we were rather than worrying about where we might be in another fifteen or twenty years. By 1995, at 65, I had retired, and five years later, with both daughters married and with grandchildren in Connecticut and Washington State, we seemed to be without a care. Judy and I were still living in the family house, but we began to think about actually retiring and downsizing. After forty years as Mid-Westerners living on the East Coast, we decided to try something new and headed to Seattle where Barb and her family lived. Our cross-country move forced us to reduce the volume of our possessions, particularly Judy's books.

We purchased a beautiful condo in the Magnolia neighborhood of Seattle in late 1999. It had a level entry but the living space was down two flights of stairs. We still considered stairs to be an interesting architectural feature rather than the physical barrier they would become. I recall seeing a flyer from a senior residential community where Barb was speaking. It prominently featured a photograph of a party of old folks around a decorated table wearing party hats. She said that Judy and I needed to count on living in the condo for ten years but after that, we'd likely need to consider a move to a congregate community. I couldn't visualize either Judy or me wearing those pointy hats, ever. And in ten years?

In 2006, Judy was examined for difficulty in swallowing and she was diagnosed with a meningioma, a typically benign brain tumor. As a child, Judy was subjected to X-radiation to shrink her tonsils. Her treatment was part of a larger study at a local Chicago Hospital where radiation was used to treat a number of ailments.[5] The radiologists in the early 40's felt that not having to subject children to that surgery was worth the hazard of the added exposure to X-rays. Judy's brother and cousins, all of whom had also received X-radiation treatments, subsequently developed medical conditions we believed were traceable back to the radiation treatment. Her brother, Joseph, developed a malignant glioblastoma at age 61 in 1998, and he died the following year.

By 2009, Judy's meningioma had grown large enough to require surgical intervention to avoid putting pressure on the brain stem, which could cause facial deformity. The meningioma was shrunk to about 20% of its original size by surgery. Following the surgery, Judy suffered

---

[5] During the years 1930-early 1960, the now-defunct Michael Reese Hospital and Medical Center in Chicago, used X-ray therapy to treat approximately 5,000 patients for certain benign conditions of the head and neck. http://articles.chicagotribune.com/2004-11-14/features/0411140458_1_butterfly-shaped-gland-thyroid-cancer-radiation;

aspiration pneumonia that left her critically ill for weeks. Eventually, she needed to have a feeding tube placed. Her extended hospitalization led to a condition the doctor labeled "post-operative delirium." Judy was so anxious that she could not be left alone and required the presence of a "constant observer" (CO) in her room at all times. Left alone, she would ring for the nurse or call out. She couldn't explain her fears, but she was visibly gripped by terror.

Her swallowing was improving and her speech had returned to normal, but the anxiety remained an issue. One day, after a month in the hospital, we were told she would be discharged to a nursing home. Barb balked and offered instead to move Judy into her house, which had a spare bedroom on the first floor and easy access to the kitchen and living spaces. We knew that Judy still needed a CO, so we hired a person to cover an 8-hour evening shift. The first night at Barb's house, the CO was so unnerved by Judy's anxiety that she woke Barb and told her she couldn't take it anymore. Barb let her go home and called me. I drove across town at 3:00 a.m., and we hatched a new plan: I would also move into Barb's home, and, with her son and our community of friends and neighbors—supplemented by outside care as needed—we'd nurse Judy back to health. I bought a whiteboard and scheduled the 27 medications she was taking. We learned how to manage the feeding-tube and its chronic computer malfunction, and we learned how to live with each other again after years of maintaining separate households. Judy's recovery took almost nine months.

I have had a lifetime of health problems caused by flat feet and varicose veins. Judy now was well, but she was not as stable as she had been. I felt a shift in the pattern of our lives. Suddenly, I was the person making plans and maintaining a social calendar. Judy had never liked driving. Post-surgery, she was not allowed to drive. That meant I would be the person shopping and taking care of daily business. In a moment, I knew that the stairs in our condominium had become a problem and that we could not continue living there.

By spring 2014, Judy had shown significant and increasing short-term memory-loss. After rounds of testing, a physician at Harborview Hospital diagnosed her with Alzheimer's Disease, and she showed us images of Judy's brain that reflected the death of some cellular material. Judy heard the diagnosis and said to Barb, "Oh, that's going to be terrible for your father." But when we were driving home, Judy asked me, "When did the doctor say I would have Alzheimer's?" I told her that the doctor had said she already had Alzheimer's. Later, Judy refused to see that doctor again because she gave her this diagnosis.

Judy was 81 years old when we learned of her diagnosis. It was as if she had been handed a death sentence without an execution date. I don't know how anyone could be prepared for this diagnosis. I certainly wasn't. Judy turned away from the things that had interested her. She couldn't follow conversations, and interrupted others with pointless comments. I was not ready for the speed with which the disease tore through my wife's body. In less than two years her illness changed her into a person unable to function. She passed away in early November 2016.

While Judy was declining, I was facing my own health issues. In early 2013, I had a replacement of the right knee. While I was recovering from surgery in the rehab unit at our care community, Judy tried to walk through the building to see me, and became lost. I realized three years later that my right hip was too painful to be ignored any longer. The hip replacement had to be done the same time Judy seemed to be slipping away. We set a surgery date of November 3, but a week before I contracted cellulitis in my legs and the surgery was canceled. I was admitted to the hospital while Judy was clinging to life. I was discharged to the Health Care Center on October 31, days before Judy passed away. I am grateful I could be there in the apartment when she died. The planned surgery didn't take place for months.

Perhaps no one could have planned for what happened in late October and November 2016. But it went as well as these things can go, and I believe that the planning we did paid off. We had done all the "right things." We had supplemental health insurance and had downsized to a continuing care community. We had the benefit of involved family who had vital support from true friends. We had medical support from the doctors who made Judy hospice-eligible and provided her with services during her last weeks of life. It has been new and different, and we have had moments of tremendous sadness and loss. But through it all, I have felt safe in my home and supported by my family and my community.

I would like every senior who reads this book to experience the kindness and consideration that marked these years for Judy and for me.

Straight Talk About Getting Old

According to a recent U.S. Census Bureau report, there are now more Americans age 65 and older (so-called "senior citizens") than at any time before in the nation's history. By 2050, 20% of the U.S. population will be 65 or older.

Rather than being a time of reward and exploration, the years over 65 are marked by health challenges and the need to spend time and money on this instead of on travel.

Age 65 and up still represents retirement age for many, although when retirement can last decades, you sometimes need to go back to work. (Or, you just get bored. As a friend who had retired at 62 complained, "Every day is Saturday!") The post-employment years are supposed to be filled with long-awaited trips to exotic locations, hours spent pursuing hobbies and reconnecting with family and friends. But too many of us know someone whose golden years were stolen or tarnished by loss—loss of good health, friends and loved ones; of vision, hearing, and mobility; of financial, physical and social independence, of hope for the future. When every step hurts, you walk more slowly and stay closer to home. You're less likely to go on an outing that involves walking around when your knees hurt; if you're used to going out with your partner but you have to go out alone because he is now too sick to go out, it may not even sound like fun to make plans. The world begins to shrink.

The average life expectancy for women is currently 81; it's 76 for men. More than 50,000 Americans are now over 100 and we are still on the upside of the Baby Boom.[6] You may look 10 years younger than you are and drive until you're 90, but if you live long enough, you or someone you love will need a joint replacement, have a heart attack, get dementia, or be felled by cancer. Even if yours is not a catastrophic diagnosis, the years take their toll as your systems weaken over time.

It can seem like a betrayal. As Steve says, everything north of the neck is fine but the southbound lanes are a wreck. You can have the heart and lungs of a person half your age and still become afflicted by a progressive, debilitating illness that gradually steals your memory, speech and executive functioning (judgment and decision-making). Clean living may help, but other than genetic blessings and a healthy dose of good luck, we're not aware of any way to guarantee that you will age gracefully and remain fully independent until the end.

Aging is complex, even more so for seniors who live alone and lack the built-in presence of another person.

---

[6] Of the 76 million babies born in the Boom Years between 1946-1964, about 65.2 million remain alive. http://www.history.com/topics/baby-boomers

Unmarried seniors also miss the financial cushion of a partner's income. Seniors who can't independently perform the necessary activities of daily living (ADLs) may literally need to depend on the "kindness of strangers" to survive. Married or single, any person who is dependent on another person is in an unequal power relationship. The resulting power imbalance leaves these dependent seniors vulnerable and susceptible to manipulation, exploitation and abuse.

Exploitation can be targeted and predatory or a casual crime of opportunity. We never thought anyone in our family would become a crime statistic. There are no registries for un-apprehended financial abusers, so it is impossible to know if the caregiver you hire has a history of abuse. Steve's older brother, Ralph, a bachelor, was ill with Parkinson's disease for a decade. In the final years of his life he lived in an assisted community, but even so, he was confined to his room and was lonely. On the recommendation of a nurse at the community, he hired a daily chore worker who helped him make purchases and do occasional errands. One day, Ralph mentioned to Steve that the care provider had threatened to quit, but had agreed to stay on if Ralph would give him a credit card for "special" purchases. This arrangement was proving satisfactory, if expensive to Ralph, and the caregiver had agreed to remain in place.

By the time we caught on to the scam, accessed the credit card statements, and cancelled the card, Ralph had withdrawn $1,500 from the bank for the caregiver. The man bought several thousand dollars worth of costume jewelry and placed numerous expensive overseas calls using Ralph's cell phone. Fortunately, the caregiver agency returned the stolen money, but the caregiver vanished before any action could be taken. Furthermore, the police declared that since Ralph had consented to the use of the card, it would be difficult to make a case against the caregiver.

We certainly never thought anyone in our family would become a crime statistic. The true breadth of the problem of elder abuse is hard to calculate because it's an issue shrouded in shame: How many people want to admit they were duped into sending money to a phony charity or they trusted a family member who wound up stealing from them? One out of every 10 seniors says he has been the victim of some form of exploitation, fraud or abuse. In 2016, there were 2.5 million crimes reported involving elder abuse, exploitation, fraud or neglect, and *only one crime out 15* against a senior was thought to be reported. The estimated loss to seniors annually is $36 billion.

None of this is meant to suggest that you can't find a way to age on your own terms, to receive care in a setting that is familiar and comfortable to you, and die free of pain and fear. You shudder at the thought of a future in congregate care. What do you envision? Whether your goal is to decamp to a 50-and-Over Fun-in-the-Sun planned community in Arizona or remain in your always impractical but oh-so-lovingly-restored Victorian home with stairs, you should *start planning now*. With mind, ears and eyes wide open, investigate what it would cost today to pay for the chores you do taking care of your home, managing your bills, and taking care of yourself. What does it cost to live in a retirement community in the place you want to retire? Go online and look at the fee schedules for home-care and fiduciary service companies. If you had surgery and needed help at home for one week, what would a week of in-home services cost? What would it cost for a month?

We're not making judgments or advocating a particular lifestyle for anyone. We're on the side of aging well and we're advocating only for safety. If the decision to live alone or to reject help is not creating physical or financial risk, then the decision is sound. If the lifestyle choices are potentially harmful to the senior or others around him, or if the decision-maker doesn't understand the consequences of his actions, then the fiduciary *must* step in. People often ask how you know when you have to step in and offer help—when the plan is unsafe and inadequate, then it's time.

This is the beginning of the most significant reality check of adulthood. The good news is that squarely facing the issues of aging now will help you identify any false assumptions in your planning. Even the most finely tuned plan can fall apart if a medical crisis develops or a financial disaster takes place. The best laid plans of mice and men, they say, often go awry, so being flexible and open to change is important. Investigate the options and set these side-by-side with your own preferences.

Understand the costs of care, and think through how long you can realistically live alone and what services can be hired. Becoming informed lets you take a realistic look at your options. Like any plan of action, a transition from independent living to any kind of care – in or out of home—will have the greatest chance of success when you're calling the shots.

The Myths Seniors Tell Themselves and Their Families:

- When I need your help, I'll let you know.
- I will live in my own home until I die.
- When I am old, ill and dying, my family will take care of me.
- When I can no longer manage my money and financial affairs, a trusted person will handle my finances.
- I don't want to do any estate planning and I don't need a will. When I die, my family will sort it out.

Myth #1: When I Need Your Help, I'll Let You Know

Old habits die hard. Intelligent, strong-willed people don't yield their personalities to dementia without a fight, although dementia always seems to win. My mom had always been proud of her ability to surprise casual listeners with a sharp or sassy comeback. One day, deep into her illness, she overheard two community residents talking about her. "Oh, don't mind Judy," one woman advised the other. "She's not really rude, she has Alzheimer's disease." The other resident sighed with understanding. Mom strode over to them on her walker and said, "I do not have Alzheimer's disease," she said, "I *am* rude."[7]

Some people are reclusive by nature. Some have never paid much attention to social norms around personal hygiene or home maintenance. We each have the right to be reclusive and anti-social. We have the right to be

---

[7] One senior client I accompanied to a doctor's appointment almost had Mom beat in the depth of character department. "So, Mrs. Smith," asked the doctor, "can you tell me your date of birth?" My client hadn't a clue about her date of birth, but men she knew, and she turned on the charm like a 100-watt bulb. "Oh Doctor," she breathed, a gowned Marilyn Monroe singing JFK a happy birthday, "don't you know a gentleman never asks a lady her age?"

eccentric, to deliberately wear mismatched socks, to insist that the powder room towels match or live in a house with a compostable toilet in a solar-powered room. We are free to reject offers of help. In theory, anyway, we have the freedom to manage our affairs in the way that suits us regardless of the judgments of others. "Society" doesn't always have the right to intervene and recommend (or insist) that a person opt for a better—read: safer—standard of living. We *are* free to live and die as we choose even if others object.

- Dave, 85, is a professor emeritus at a local university. Long divorced, he owns a beautiful home with a view, where he and a succession of dogs have happily lived, until now. Dave recently had both knees replaced and going up and down the stairs poses a safety risk. He had a lengthy stay at rehab and is camped out on the first floor of his home. Dave's son has asked him to think about relocating to a senior community. Dave likes his privacy and fears that he will have nothing in common with the other retirees, but he tells himself he will think it over.

  One afternoon Dave walks down the drive to collect his mail and collapses in a heap. He's undergone a heart attack and is not moving. His dog, Seashell, sits down next to him and naps, but as evening comes, the dog gets hungry and begins to whimper. Her whimpers turn sharper and louder, until sometime later in the evening the neighbors report the disturbance to the police. When the police find him, Dave has been dead for several hours.

Some seniors lack the ability to provide for their own needs due to a physical disability or mental impairment. Diminished capacity and poor judgment are often the result of dementia. The senior would, if he could, secure wholesome food, clean, appropriate clothes, and medical care. When the choices are conscious, it's a lifestyle choice. The problem is when the person making the decisions is too ill to understand the choices. Senior self-neglect is often referred to as a "silent epidemic" because an increasing number of seniors are failing to thrive. The situation is compounded by the difficulty social service providers have locating and serving this population.

In a report of the American Society on Aging[8] 92 percent of care managers surveyed found self-neglecting elders to be a significant and largely unreported problem in their communities. More than 3/4 of the care managers reported that third-party neglect of seniors was the most common non-financial form of elder abuse/neglect they encountered.

---

[8] The National Adult Protective Services Association (NAPSA) defines self- neglect as, "an adult's inability, due to physical or mental impairment or diminished capacity, to perform essential self- care...."http://asaging.org/blog/elder- self-neglect-growing-and-largely- hidden-problem

- Ted is 92. A bachelor and former university professor, he taught art history until arthritis forced him to retire. He has lived for the last 40 years in a small home on a wooded lot. Ted leaned politically libertarian as a younger man and always had fears about government power. As his dementia has advanced, his fears have deepened into paranoia. He has many fears. He believes that people are coming into his house. Ted doesn't open his mail, and he hasn't seen the notices from the County that his real property taxes are delinquent. When he neglected to pay his water and electric bills, those utility services were terminated. A few months ago, the City condemned the house and ordered that it be razed. Fines have been imposed and are accumulating daily against the property for Ted's failure to comply with the City's orders. Since then he has been living out of his car which is parked in the front yard.

Ted's neighbors have complained about the condition of the home and yard. He won't pay the utility bills, so he has no garbage or recycling services. Trash is piled up around the house and stashed in the car. Ted is afraid of "rays" that he believes penetrate his mind, and he is seen walking around the City in a tented hat and breastplate fashioned from cardboard and remnants of aluminum foil. Ted's home has no running water or functioning plumbing and his neighbors are concerned that he is relieving himself in their yards and in public spaces where their children play, creating a potentially dangerous public health situation.

When a neighbor reports her concerns about Ted to the local office of Adult Protective Services ("APS"), which investigates, it finds Ted to be "at risk," and files a petition to establish a court-supervised guardianship..

It's complicated to know just where the right of an impaired senior to live freely stops. That line is clearly drawn when a senior's impaired thinking creates a risk of harm to others. A condominium owner with hoarding behavior can load the rooms with books until the rooms are impassable. But he crosses the line when he stores moldy food that creates a vermin infestation in the community storage area. It's the same with a driver's license. Seniors have the right to drive long after they can safely handle a car. That right may not be curtailed unless someone sees the senior driving erratically and reports it to the Department of Motor Vehicles or the senior is involved in an accident.

- Carol, 73, is a wealthy widow. She lives in a spacious condominium that her son, Bob, encouraged her to buy after her husband died. Without her husband's influence, Carol's shopping demon has been unleashed. A postal delivery service arrives almost daily with new purchases, and Carol attends a weekly auction where she purchases a "lot"— a grab bag of more items requiring storage. The

> condo's two bedrooms are filled with her purchases still in their unopened boxes.
>
> Never much of a cook and a notoriously picky eater, Carol eats out all the time. She parks her leftovers in the refrigerators and lets them turn moldy. The food in her cabinets is no better. Packages of old dried fruit provided a breeding ground for gnats, and the kitchen had to be exterminated. Carol left bread sitting out until it went bad. Bob threw it away, but the next day he discovered that Carol had retrieved the ancient crust from the garbage.
>
> One night when Bob stops by, the smoke detector is wailing and he sees smoke in the kitchen. When Carol seems oblivious to the smell and the noise, he rushes past her into the kitchen and finds a waxed paper cup burning on the stovetop.

Seniors who previously managed quite well may find their rational thinking clouded by grief over the loss of a loved one or anxiety over health, family or money worries. They may be in denial of their health or financial situation, and due to failing cognition, they may lack any true insight into their needs. Some will have trouble finding in-home help or securing government assistance because of language or cultural barriers and a corresponding lack of familiarity with the American medical system. Some seniors hesitate to ask for help because they fear they will become a burden to their friends and families or because they believe that needing help is a sign weakness. Some partners make promises to care for each other that, for many reasons, they just can no longer fulfill. Still others may find caregivers who enable them in their denial by being willing to pick up after them and make excuses.

- Bart, 84, and Jeannine, 82, have been married for 30 years. A second marriage for each, they are devoted to one another and live in her beautiful home with a view. They have hired help to clean the house and prepare meals, but Bart is still his wife's caretaker. Jeannine has Lewy Body Disease, a, progressive dementia that affects movement, balance and memory, and can cause delusions and hallucinations. The spouses, whose children live at a distance in other states, promised each other long that neither would ever go into a care facility.

  Jeannine's medications keep her complacent but sometimes she argues and resists taking her pills. One night at pill-taking time, Bart tries to cajole Jeannine, but she refuses, suddenly swiveling her head away. Already tired, Bart attempts to get Jeannine to open her mouth, but he is overly rough, shoving the glass a little too hard. The glass breaks, cutting Jeannine's lip. Startled by the stinging pain, Jeannine pulls away from Bart, loses her balance and falls to the floor, striking the back of her head on the sharp edge of the granite countertop.

  The next day, the housekeeper finds blood on Jeannine's pillow and observes her matted hair. She calls the police and Bart is arrested on suspicion of domestic abuse.

The Reality: You Won't Know When You Will Need Help.

One day at work, I received this email:

> I am the eldest of six siblings, and we are in desperate need of advice. Our father is a very strong-willed, independent man who raised us with an iron hand. Now his health is deteriorating and we think he may have dementia. None of us know how to talk to him about hiring some help around the house. I try to call him every day, but sometimes I can't reach him. I know he often lets my calls go to voicemail. When I do get a chance to speak with him directly and I try to ask about repairs he is supposed to make to the house or whether he's current on the bills, he changes the subject.
>
> Dad is ashamed of the condition of his home but can't get organized enough to call for repairs. His bedroom has been unlivable since mom died—filled with boxes of her papers and clothes. He falls asleep on the living room couch in his clothes. I think sometimes he does not change his clothes or bathe for days; he looks ragged when I visit, and he's stopped shaving. He does not cook and I'm worried that he is not eating well; I am also not certain he is taking his prescription medicines properly.

Since Mom died, Dad is drinking and driving again. Some of the bars he frequents will now only serve him one drink; others have quit serving him altogether. One night, getting out of his car in a parking lot, Dad fell and couldn't get up. Medics were called. Seeing that he was intoxicated, they drove him home. When he slipped going into the house and he couldn't stand up, the medics took him to the hospital. A blood alcohol reading placed him substantially above the legal blood-alcohol limit.

No matter how hard we try, Dad just pushes us away and says he doesn't need any help. We are worried that he is in danger of harming himself and afraid that his finances are a wreck.

Do you have any suggestions?

It's heartbreaking: You owe your parents so much of what you have learned in life and all that you can see you have inherited directly: Your red hair or blue eyes, your resourcefulness and intelligence, your cultural heritage and religious affiliation, a favorite cake recipe or the carving knife that your dad inherited from his father, and that has cut into decades of your family's Thanksgiving turkeys. Now your senior parent is experiencing physical decline or dementia and is making decisions that are ill-considered or even dangerous. How do you show the ailing parent your love and respect for his self- determination when he is making decisions that could cause him harm? And most important, how do you know when you have waited long enough and need to do something?

We have already established that every person has the right to fail – that is, live in filthy clothes and in unsafe conditions. No one can force an unwilling party to accept care services, take prescribed medications or attend a doctor's appointment. Parent-child relationships are powerful and adult children still fear the displeasure of their parents; telling their senior that he can't go home from the hospital alone may be the first time the child has ever been in the position of saying no to his parent.

Yes, you can—you should—honor your senior and acknowledge his right to independence. You can also acknowledge to yourself that this person is ill and doesn't truly understand what they are saying. It's crazy-making, because the person refusing to listen or acknowledge reality looks like and sounds like the person you have always known. It's just that they don't respond in the ways that you have come to expect. In the myriad ways you expect them to *be*, they are altered. I tried to explain to Steve how I had come to think about my mom—the times we were together that could be so trying, the episodes he recounted when she acted oddly or jettisoned plans to go to an event they had happily attended dozens of times before, leaving him in a lurch.. I tried to explain how I had come to think about it. "Dad, she looks like Mom and she sounds like Mom, but the aliens took her away long ago. The person you're talking to is a shell; she's a pod person from 'The

Invasion of the Body Snatchers.' That woman at the table is *not* Judy Adler." It was just my way of lessening the sadness I'd experienced after seeing how little she could do or understand—but it was absolutely true. If you let yourself think you are dealing with the person you used to know, you are asking to be frustrated.

You have to steel yourself, armed with legal authority, to speak truth to power, that is, the parent you were raised to obey. As a responsible care provider, you are concerned that the senior is not getting the right kind of care and you are certain that the senior isn't accurately reporting his symptoms, needs, and medication compliance to you or to the medical providers. You are fairly certain that when you ask your senior questions, he will get mad and may even throw you out of the house. But honestly, how long is the senior going to stay mad at you? You're the helper, the caregiver. *You have the power – if you will use it--to force reasonable changes for the purpose of safety.*

They mean well, but social service and medical professionals who advise caregivers to "have the conversation" with their seniors about their needs aren't providing a useful strategy. Arguing or trying to rationalize with a person through the scrim of dementia is an exercise in futility. My mom needed eye surgery, and my dad and I spent hours discussing this with her. Her doctor recommended the operation and cautioned that waiting would make the procedure more risky and might make the outcome less favorable. We explained, each of us, how important it was and how devastating it would be for her to lose her sight. "I don't like him," she said to my dad. I butted in, sure I could help. I reminded her that this doctor had been referred by her physician, whom she *did* like. I spoke about the benefits of surgery and the potential for problems if she waited. I liked the doctor, I reassured her. I was certain he would do the operation successfully. She eyed me. "If you think it is such a good idea," she said, "then why don't you have the operation?" and she went back to her ice cream.

If you believe that your senior is at risk of harming himself or a third party, you can try to bring help into the home or work with your senior to consider relocating to a residential community. In extreme cases you may need to petition for a guardianship (conservatorship) or you can ask a Court to issue an order under a power of attorney allowing you to override specific decisions made by the senior. In some jurisdictions you can file a petition for the protection of a vulnerable adult if the senior is harming herself, or you can seek an injunction against a third party who is unduly influencing or acting against the best interests of the senior.

You may try to address your senior's care needs in what seems a more democratic way, offering suggestions for in-home help, out-of-home options and everything you can think of in between. Imagine how frustrating it is to come up with all of these ideas just to have the senior reject it all as unnecessary, overly-complicated and too expensive. The ugly truth is that the senior who needs help but refuses to accept it is holding her family hostage to her illness. The senior who seeks to remain independent when that is no longer feasible literally tethers her caregivers to her by fear and guilt. Although she maintains that she does not want to be a burden and wants to be—can be—self-supporting, she actually is making her caregivers' responsibility more difficult. Everyone is now interdependent and cannibalizing their resources just to make it through one more day until a catastrophe occurs that forces a decision to be made.

When you're working with seniors, the "children" can be well into their 60s. It is always a surprise to find that adult children are afraid of their parents. The child, no doubt well-disciplined from an early age, knows his parent's personal and psychological boundaries and can anticipate the reaction that will come when *the parents* are told they need help now. I've seen surgeons, judges and real estate magnates quake at the thought of their ancient mothers being angry with them for taking a stand and demanding (the nerve!) they get proper care.

Even more serious challenges can arise when the senior becomes affected by severe anxiety and paranoia. In those cases, the child, who in healthy times would have been a resource now becomes an adversary, challenging the senior's right to reject medical help decent meals and efforts at cleaning, repairing or simply organizing a home to make it comfortable.

In the interest of full disclosure, the authors of this book are also parents, and advocate proper child discipline. ("You want to raise your child so that someone *other* than you will like them," Judy would have said.) But it is not reasonable for a parent to expect even the best-behaved child to stand by silently as he declines physically and mentally. Think of it this way: You have to allow your child to be the person you have raised him to be. That is, conscientious, mature and perceptive.

Tools for the Caregiver: Powers of Attorney

What can you do if your senior is refusing help but is clearly in need?

1. **Legal Arrangements**. If your senior does not yet have powers of attorney in place and he has the ability to form a working relationship with a lawyer, you need to locate an estate planning or elder law attorney in your community and schedule an appointment to *get these documents prepared and signed.*[9] A **power of attorney** provides legal authority for an "agent" to act for a "principal." In an era of heightened protection of confidential information, durable powers of attorney for health care and finances are tools when one person is managing another's finances or health care.

    a) **Finding a Lawyer**. If you can't get a referral to an attorney from a friend or adviser, you can check your State Association for online attorney listings. State and County Bar Associations sponsor "Senior Clinics" and may offer estate planning services at no cost ("pro bono), low-cost or on a sliding scale pegged to income. The National Academy of Elder Law Attorneys (http://www.naela.org), has members in the

---

[9] It may be tempting to go to an online source and create them yourself to save money; **resist the urge!** It is not legal for a non-attorney to practice law without a license, and if you are drafting a legal document for a third party, you are acting as a lawyer.

US, Canada, UK, and Australia and offers a state-by-state registry of its membership. Most larger cities have a Senior Services Department that may be able to provide referrals to local Senior Services providers.

b) **Meeting the Lawyer.** Generally, the person who brings the senior to the office is asked to wait outside while the attorney meets the client and assesses his capacity to enter into an attorney/client relationship. A client's relationship with an attorney is privileged, so all communications between them are strictly confidential. If a third party is present at an attorney-client meeting, the privilege is broken, except in the case of older clients. If a person is at a meeting to assist the senior, then that person's presence *does not* affect the confidential nature of the communications.

2. **Powers of Attorney.** A durable power of attorney may be either immediate or springing. The **immediate durable power of attorney** is effective upon signing. The **springing durable power of attorney** goes into effect after a specific event occurs, such as a when a doctor certifies that the principal is medically incapacitated.

a) A **durable** power of attorney specifically allows the agent to continue to act on the principal's behalf after he becomes incapacitated. For this reason, durable powers of attorney are preferred when assisting seniors.

3. **The Fiduciary**
   a) A person who has been appointed as an agent for a **principal** under a power of attorney is a **fiduciary**. A fiduciary owes the duty of absolute loyalty to his principal and must treat the principal with utmost fealty. Without a power of attorney in place it will be difficult, if not impossible, for you to exercise your client's right to receive personal medical and financial information, which is a vital part of your role.
   b) An agent/fiduciary who has accepted appointment has an **affirmative duty — responsibility**—to the principal to **protect** him from harm and **preserve** his estate. The agent can hire other people to help him perform his duties to the senior. If the principal is injured as a result of the agent's failure to act (neglect) or by the agent's reckless or willful conduct, the agent can be required to reimburse the principal for any losses incurred by the agent's failure of duty.
      i) An agent for a senior who is capacitated but self-neglecting can offer help but generally has no authority to override the decisions of the principal.
      ii) An agent for a senior who has witnessed over time that the senior cannot manage his personal, medical and residential needs should take steps to bring the needed services to the senior.

4. **Non-Legal Resources**
   a) **Call 911.** Although they are not a social service agency, if you can't reach a senior after trying and are worried about their safety, you can call 911 and ask the police to do a wellness check on a senior. If too many of these are reported, the police may take it upon themselves to call APS and ask them to investigate whether or not it would be appropriate to begin a guardianship proceeding.

   b) **Call the Doctor.** When all else fails, take your non-compliant senior to an emergency room. A doctor can admit a patient for observation, testing and treatment, and then permit discharge only when a suitable care plan— reviewed by a care professional—is in place. When a doctor won't allow a patient to be discharged until there is care in place, the argument is won (at least for the moment).

   c) **Call the local office of Adult Protective Services (APS).** Adult Protective Services is an arm of every state's Department of Social and Health Services, which is charged in part with the protection of vulnerable citizens. Anyone can make an anonymous referral to begin the process of investigation, and all referrals remain anonymous.

Myth #2: I Will Live In My Own Home Until I Die.

A mother/son team came in to see me one day about estate planning. She moved slowly with her 4-wheeled walker. We sat down and she stayed silent, looking to her son to do the talking. (Over the years I've learned that this is usually a clue that the senior is experiencing memory loss.) The son opened the conversation, stating, "Mom is having some memory problems and I feel she needs help to be safe at home, but we aren't sure how to accomplish this. Mom doesn't believe in Medicaid because she thinks it's Welfare. Selling the house is not an option because I intend to live there with my family when Mom's gone. She doesn't understand that she has to pay for help around the house. And we are just not going to discuss having her go to some residential community." Then he stopped and thought for a moment. "One more thing," he advised, "she doesn't want strangers in her home."

I was stumped, because it seemed that unless the plan was for the son to move in and provide care himself, he had just taken all the planning options off the table.

In 26 years as a lawyer, I have never had a single client express a desire to die in a nursing home. Everyone wants to die in his sleep in the place we call home, free of pain and fear, with someone they trust close at hand. "Moving is an Adventure" is a great corporate slogan for U-rent trailers, but when you are tired, in pain, alone, depressed and anxious about the future the complexity of relocating may be so overwhelming that it becomes paralyzing. There is good reason why seniors dig in their heels with particular ferocity on this issue.

Despite the desires of people to die at home, more people are dying in health-care institutions over the last century. Twenty-five percent of all deaths today take place in nursing homes, and the proportion of all deaths that occur in these settings continues to rise. By 2020, it's estimated that 40% of Americans will die in a skilled nursing facility. It seems reasonable that a factor in increased demand for institutional nursing care is the rise in persons living alone who can't meet their care needs at home.

Although living alone was virtually unknown in most world cultures prior to the 20th century, it is currently estimated that, in the U.S., 32.7 million people, or about 12% of the nation's households, live alone.[10] While all generalizations are dangerous, single seniors tend to be at greater risk for financial challenges later in life without the cushion of spouse or partner's income and benefits. Singles generally experience difficulty receiving care while convalescing at home because they lack the assistance of family. Couples have their unique complications—the physical and

---

[10] https://www.nia.nih.gov/research/publication/global-health-and-aging/living-longer.

emotional dependence of the couple and role reversal that often accompanies terminal illness; complex dynamics and conflicts of interest with children and competition within families for control of the seniors and their finances.

Regardless of your marital status, reaching the decision that you need help and should relocate or bring care into your home is a life-altering decision. In fact, the thought of what a move will entail may simply stop you in your tracks, until a disaster occurs. Now your partner needs to have 24-hour help, which you can't afford, and you can't delay moving any longer. Imagine you and your spouse delayed moving after he retired 20 years ago because the thought of sorting through your married lifetime of belongings overwhelmed you. How will you get the boxes and packing material? Now you're 85; your arthritic hands throb with pain and you have neuropathy in your feet. The thought of tackling the mess in the storage room certainly isn't going to be any more appealing now than it was then. How will you ever decide what goes where?

Then there's the daunting prospect of establishing a new social identity— becoming acquainted with an unfamiliar neighborhood and new neighbors. How would a senior feel about moving into a care community if his partner isn't mobile any longer or is exhibiting bizarre behavior? How do you make new friends when you spend all of your time apologizing for the inappropriate remarks your partner has made? When Judy and Steve first relocated to their care community, Judy was much the same person she had always been. Over time, though, the illness altered Judy's personality in ways that created socially awkward situations. She acted strangely when they were at dinner with others and spoke out of turn at meetings. She criticized people for speaking too loudly or walking too slowly. Steve tried as hard as he could for as long as he could to maintain a normal social life. As the problem deepened, Steve "lost" his social partner of 60 years. He sometimes said (only joking a little) that he felt like the fellow who trails after the circus elephant, cleaning up the mess. Steve had support from an extended community of family and friends, and he had the benefit of a sense of humor. But not every person whose partner is changing can understand what is motivating the changes or coping with them.

No wonder people want to stay at home.

This is where duty and obligation come in. By law, spouses have a legal duty to take care of each other. If your spouse is failing medically, you must get him help unless he tells you he does not want care. Because of the mutual duty inherent in the marital relationship, failing to make sure that your spouse gets appropriate care is legal abandonment. There's no problem wanting to stay at home until you die as long as you have a care plan that is (1) sustainable, (2) safe and (3) does not increase the likelihood that you will become a target for exploitation.

Is Your Plan Practical and Sustainable?

- George, 92, and Mary, 90, live in the home where they raised their children. They are adamant about remaining in their home, surrounded by their memories. Mary is legally blind. George has mild congestive heart failure and trouble with swelling in his legs. They live on a modest income of two small pensions and Social Security, and they pay a neighbor to provide a few hours of household help each week. Mary stays in bed most of the day because if she falls, George can't help her.

George manages the calendar of medical appointments for Mary and himself and also manages their medications; recently he found that he had missed a few dosages. Even with some help, George is fatigued lately and feels overwhelmed by running the household. The groceries now come by delivery, but the laundry, yard work and house repairs, are done by the couple's sons, who arrive each weekend to help as much as they can. The daughters-in-law are beginning to grumble and one son has suggested that he can't come over this week.

Is Your Plan Safe?

- Shirley was widowed at a young age and has always lived with her only daughter, June. The years have not been kind to June. She was a young beauty, but started drinking in her 40s to blunt the loneliness of being the wife of a workaholic and serial philanderer. Her looks faded and her behavior became a not-very private source of embarrassment as the children grew older. June's run-ins with inebriated fender benders has long been fodder for local gossips. June's husband, a prominent cosmetic dentist, eventually left her for a winsome dental assistant. The kids took their father's side in the split.

Shirley and June rattle around in the family home. June has daytime household help and they also assist Shirley. Lately, Shirley has become increasingly dependent upon June for care, but June is often too drunk to cook dinner or help with Shirley's evening bath. June smokes and has a history of falling asleep with a cigarette burning between her fingers. Her forearms are also marked by burns. Recently, she tried to stay sober but after two days was so shaky and nauseated that she dropped a pan of hot sauce and was splattered and burned by the bubbling liquid.

One night, Shirley attempts to take a shower and falls in the tub. She calls to her daughter for help, but June is passed out in the living room and doesn't respond. Shirley has fallen on her arm and can't move. The hot water tank runs out and she is sprayed with cold water. She lies there all night until the daytime help arrives and finds her.

Will your plan make you a target for exploitation?

- Alex is 85, his wife, Clara is 84. A diabetic, Alex long ago lost both legs below the knee and uses a wheelchair. Clara has advanced Alzheimer's disease. The couple have two children, Grant and

Donna. One sunny June afternoon, Alex loses control of the car he drives with hand controls. He and Clara are hospitalized and the discharge plan requires that they get in-home help or relocate to a care community.

Donna lives hours away; Grant lives near his parents. He has never provided care to anyone before, but his lease is ending soon and he needs to relocate; this is a good interim plan. He agrees to move in with Alex and Clara to care for them. Grant proposes that he act as a caregiver, housekeeper and personal driver, and he asks to be paid $60,000 annually for his services. Donna is relieved that her parents will have the help they need, and she agrees to let Grant take charge.

When Grant moves in, he quickly makes changes. After taking care of Clara for only a few days, he realizes the extent of her needs and moves her into a memory care community. Grant moves Alex downstairs into a windowless storeroom behind the garage. He claims the master bedroom suite for himself and a smaller room for his son. He takes Clara's clothes to the dump. Grant disassembles the stair climber that has allowed Alex to freely access the home's multiple levels despite being a paraplegic.

Over the next six months, Grant uses his parents' checking account to buy himself new shop tools and clothing. He adds premium channels to Alex and Clara's cable subscription and sets up a family plan of cell phones for his children. Grant sifts through his parents' belongings and packs up the china and crystal to send to his eldest daughter. Always dissatisfied with his parents' kitchen, and assuming that he will live at the house from now on, Grant tears out the dining room wall to start a remodel and orders new appliances. He decides to re-carpet the upstairs and hires his son to do the installation.

In December, Donna comes to town and finds her mother gone, her father a virtual prisoner in the basement, and the upstairs of the home in total disarray. Grover has spent almost $200,000 of his parents' savings in six months.

The Reality: You May be Unsafe at Home.

Myth #2 is a corollary to *Dying At Home*. It's also not unreasonable, if you first acknowledge these realities:

1. Most likely, the senior does not have a family member who is going to drop his life to move in and take care of him.
2. If the senior has a partner, there is no guarantee which of the two will live longer and which one will stay healthy. Neither one may be able to be a caregiver for the other when the time comes.

   One (1) plus Two (2) = Three (3).
3. That is, the senior will have to pay for his care.

Suppose you want to go from Florida to Niagara Falls in late June, the height of the tourist season. You don't just pack a suitcase, lock the front door and show up at the airport. You arrange for flights, a rental car and a hotel room, and maybe even e-tickets for a ride on the *Maid of The Mist*. Most people can't simply stay in their homes and continue to do all the things that are needed until the day they die. For the overwhelming number of seniors, choosing to age in place means that now or later, at some point, you will need to bring help in or move out of your home.

Tools for the Caregiver: Thinking Through Home-Based Care

A home-based care plan is a written document that sets out important information regarding the senior's current medical condition, social and emotional needs, and the steps that are *going* to be taken to meet them.[11] The care plan is developed based on the senior's historic expressed wishes and desires, tempered with the reality of his or her financial situation.

Home-based care requires substantially more money than living in a senior community. The senior must have enough money to pay for necessary care, plus the costs of owning a home. In some cases the home will need renovations to make it safe and accessible for a senior who now uses a walker; it may also need renovations to make a new accessible bathroom and a proper space for an overnight caregiver. After the financial analysis has been completed, the senior's dream of home-based care may simply be unattainable.[12]

---

[11] http://caregiverresourcecenter.com/advanced_elder_care_planning.htm, last viewed 8/5/2017. The Caregiver Resource Center website provides a guide to developing a comprehensive care plan and resources for researching, evaluating and buying assistive equipment of all kinds. Http://caregiverresourcecenter. com/advanced_elder_care_planning.htm; See also http://www.caregiverstress.com/home-care/hospital-to-homecare/home-care-plan.

[12] Independent living communities, generally catering to people 55 and older, can be a viable alternative to staying in one's own home. The seniors in these communities maintain their own apartments and continue to live as they like, but with a daily "check in" call and more significant help as needed.

Components of a Home-Based Care Plane

Financial Component

You must have a complete understanding of the senior's finances, including all sources— monthly income, ongoing expenses, existing debts and any other financial resources that may be available.

You may want to consult an elder law attorney or a tax specialist with regard to these questions:

- Is the senior's income sufficient to manage the cost of living at home according to the budget you have prepared?
- Is there a projected shortfall of income? How will this be covered?
- Is liquidating assets to pay for ongoing costs a sustainable plan for the senior, given his age and medical condition?
- Are the senior's funds properly invested to maximize income and minimize income taxation?
- Could the senior qualify for home healthcare services through Medicare, private health insurance or Medicaid?
- Does the senior have supplemental health care insurance?
- What are the going rates for in-home care in your region?

- If the plan is to hire help in the home through a professional agency, how many hours can the senior afford at current rates?
- How long will the senior's money hold out if care needs and costs increase?
- If you are planning to manage the process of staffing care at home, what will you do if the provider calls in sick?
- How will you calculate, pay and properly report the costs of the employer's portion of Social Security, Medicare and federal income tax?

Housing Component

The housing plan must address the expenses of home modification and the ongoing costs of housing, food, taxes, insurance, utilities, and the cost of the in-home care that will be provided. To determine whether the home-based care plan as established is feasible, you need to create a proposed monthly/annual budget detailing the senior's expenses—housing, insurance, property taxes, food, utilities, out-of-pocket medical expenses (medication, co-pays, premiums for insurance), medical caregivers, housekeepers, yard maintenance, home maintenance, transportation services, and on and on.

Consider these issues:

- What specific changes must be made to the home to make it safe?
- How much will the renovations cost?

- How long will the renovations take?
- How will the cost of renovations be paid?
- Who will supervise the renovations?
- Can the senior remain in the home during the renovations?
- If the senior plans to remain at home, who will provide care services and respite care?
- What accommodations need to be made at home for the caregiver?
- If the senior cannot remain at home during this work, where will he go? What will this lodging cost?
- Will the senior be able to afford the costs associated with increasing levels of care and increasing hours of care services?

Health Component

The written healthcare plan becomes the primary tool by which the senior's family communicates with one another and the health professionals to make sure the senior's needs are being met. It sets out information regarding chronic medical conditions and current complications, identifies medical providers, details medication dosages, and includes contact information and schedules of care providers, occupational or physical therapists, bath aides and nursing services. The care plan identifies the senior's designated healthcare agent and the family, friends, professional caregivers and others who contribute to the senior's ability to live independently.

The process of developing a geriatric care plan should always begin with a professional assessment of the senior's medical status. Like the warning about creating your own estate documents, we don't advise you to make your own assessment. Unless you are a registered nurse or have credentials related to medicine and geriatric care, you probably don't have the necessary skills, and your lack of objectivity with regard to the subject is likely to affect your analysis. Your senior's physician's office should be able to make a referral for this purpose if they cannot do the assessment themselves.

You must prepare to meet the senior's **existing** and **emerging** need for medical, dental, vision and mental health care, as you address these issues:

Safety Component

- What is the senior's current health status? Diagnosis? Prognosis?
- Can the senior safely live alone? Can he call 911?
- Is the senior oriented to place and time?
- If the senior fell, would he know what to do?
- If there was a fire, would the senior safely leave the residence by himself?
- Would he recall where the doors are located?
- Would he be safe waiting outside for help to arrive?

Daily Care Component

- Does the senior need assistance to ambulate?

- Is the senior a fall risk?
- Does he use or need to use an assistive device to improve balance?
- Does the senior need assistance in transfering from bed to standing, etc.?
- Does the senior need cuing to manage activities of daily living —bathing, toileting, dressing?
- Does the senior need assistance with the activities of daily living—bathing, toileting, dressing, eating, food preparation, housekeeping, laundry?
- Does the senior need a daily phone call to check on medications and other needs?

Health Services Component

- Are professional nursing services needed?
- Are doctors' orders in place for home-based services?
- Does the senior receive home-based occupational or physical therapy services?
- Does the senior need special equipment?

Health Care/Medication Management Component

- Can the senior manage his own daily medications?
- Can the senior manage medication refills and related insurance questions?
- Can the senior drive himself to medical appointments?

- Can the senior maintain his own calendar for procedures and appointments?
- Is the senior compliant with doctors' orders?

Behavior Component

- Does the senior "exit seek" or wander? Are safety precautions in place?
- Does the senior engage in assaultive or combative conduct that would create a threat to caregivers?
- Is the senior a danger to himself?

Myth #3: When I Am Old, Ill And Dying, My Family Will Take Care Of Me.

We don't want to burden one another, but, if you get sick, you want the people closest to you to provide care. It makes sense to look at your loved ones as the people who will be most willing and able to help. (After all, my mom would have said, "Why else did you have children?") The problem is that not every member of every family is available or has the personality or skills to be a caregiver, and not every family relationship is well-served by making the parties dependent upon each other.

The same factors that make seniors resistant to even discussing congregate care underlie the wish to receive care at home. You can add to this "Worry Stew" the impact of diminished, deteriorating health. Everyone, it seems, has seen patients in an old-style nursing home and fears being "warehoused."

Receiving a diagnosis of a progressive, debilitating and possibly terminal disease is terrifying. You're facing your mortality and you may fear that in addition to being in pain, debilitated and dependent, you'll run out of money. There is a perception that home-based care is a less expensive option than moving into a residential community – if you have been thinking about making a move and now will have to go through that process feeling ill, it's no wonder people think they should just stay at home. Single seniors who have reached the limits of their ability to manage, may now seek governmental medical assistance

Cultural attitudes vary about a family's responsibilities toward its elderly members. In Asian and in Hispanic cultures, the responsibility for elder care lies firmly within the family and the expectation to receive home care is ingrained.[13] This is vastly different from the approach in the U.S. and Canada, where seniors are more likely to remain independent of their families. Although it is common for the family to intervene if an elderly relative needs help, providing daily, in-home care for an ailing senior is a challenge. More women are working outside the home, eliminating a natural pool of caregiving labor. There are more and more people living in uncoupled households.

As with the decision to stay at home for now, the decision to remain at home and receive care implicates the senior's entire family and can have decidedly mixed results.

Is Your Plan Safe?

- Geneva, 79, lived alone in her home until recently. She wants to live out her years in her home. Her

---

[13] https://opentextbc.ca/introductiontosociology/chapter/chapter13-aging-and-the-elderly/ last viewed 5/12/2017.

sons are busy with their own lives, but one daughter, Betty, has volunteered to move into Geneva's house along with Geneva's granddaughter, Amy, and Amy's toddler daughters. Betty's husband has a criminal history as a drug dealer and is a registered sex offender. Amy is a recovering addict with hoarding behaviors, and she also has a restraining order against Betty's husband, her stepfather, but he visits the house regularly anyway.

Amy takes over the basement of the house and fills it. Her belongings begin to creep into the main part of the home. Betty's husband takes up residence in the house and his friends stop by at all hours of the day and night to make drug deals. One night after Geneva has gone to bed, there is a brawl outside her bedroom window and shots are fired.

Some seniors expect to receive the same care that was provided to the generation ahead of them, at home. It is unthinkable that an elderly person would be sent away to receive care. The right to age in place with family care is inherent. The danger arises when no one has the necessary skills to be a caregiver.

- Marie is 75. She has congestive heart failure, high blood pressure and diabetes. She lives with her youngest daughter, Rose, who has never married and has lived at home with her mother her entire adult life. Rose is an alcoholic who suffers blackouts. Rose doesn't work and uses her mother's income to support her drinking habit. Marie's other children live out-of-state. They don't want Rose taking care of Marie and regularly ask Marie to come and live with them. Marie refuses to leave her home. She doesn't admit to Rose that her legs are getting terribly swollen and painful; she's afraid Rose will decide she is too much work and send her to a nursing home.

One day, Rose goes on a bender and leaves Marie alone over a weekend. Marie doesn't eat or drink properly and forgets to take her medications, suffering a stroke while Rose is gone. When Rose arrives home and finds Marie unresponsive, she calls for an ambulance. Marie is revived, but medical personnel suspect she may have suffered brain damage, and she needs to be admitted to a skilled nursing home for care.

Is Your Plan Sustainable?

- Jean and Jill were raised by their Aunt Trixie. Trixie is now 95, with advanced dementia, loss of vision and hearing. Trixie is bed-bound and requires round-the-clock care. Now retired women themselves, Jean and Jill have always vied for Trixie's attention and affection. Jill never married and made her home with Trixie, much to Jean's unhappiness. Jean is happily married, a mother and grandmother. She is well-off financially, but she can't shake a lifetime habit of competing with Jill.

She resents her sister's close relationship to their aunt. Jean is afraid that Trixie loves Jill more than she loves her and fears that Trixie will favor Jill with a larger share of Trixie's estate.

One day, Jill gets a call from Adult Protective Service regarding Trixie. An anonymous report has been called in that Jill is not administering Trixie's medications properly. An investigation ensues and it is determined that Jill has in fact not been giving Trixie one of her regular medications. It turns out that Jean was the anonymous tipster. The reason that Jill has not been giving Trixie this medications is that Jean has taken the pill bottle out of the home and secreted it in order to create a case against Jill for elder abuse.

Will living at home make you a target for exploitation?

- Joe, 82, a decorated career U.S. Army officer, receives a substantial pension and is entitled to free medical services at the local Veteran's Administration hospital. He has dementia and recently suffered a stroke that has left him unable to form words. A womanizer, long divorced from his wife, he recently moved into an apartment with his oldest son, Tom, and Tom's wife. Tom tells his siblings that because he has an Internet business and works from home, he can care for Joe. His siblings are all busy and live out-of-state, and they trust Tom.

Tom creates a power of attorney on the Internet and presents it to Joe at breakfast one day. The document allows Tom to manage Joe's health care and finances. It provides that while he is serving as his father's agent, Tom has the right to use Joe's assets for Joe's expenses as well as for his own. Joe is not clear about what is contained in the document, but he trusts Tom and he signs the document.

Tom believes it is fair to charge Joe a fee for caretaking services every month, but he never discusses this with Joe. Tom has always sympathized with his brother, Jack, who bore the brunt of Joe's bad temper when they were boys. Jack's life has always been rocky and he has never succeeded at much. Always his brother's Number One Fan, Tom takes out a credit card for Jack using Joe's name and credit history. Jack is full of resentment at his father and his siblings and he goes on an online spending spree. Just as Tom is learning about Jack's credit card use, his oldest sister asks what the plan is for Joe's long-term care and about the condition of his finances. When Tom tells her Joe has no money and has amassed credit card debt, she calls the police.

Do Your Loved Ones Have the Necessary Skills to Provide Care?

- Don is 83. He is a bachelor who has always been fiercely independent. He refused to sign a power of attorney when he was younger and in good health because he feared someone would use this to take away control of his money and property. Don's great-niece, Nia, lives with Don and provides care to him as needed. When Don becomes too ill to manage his needs, his brother, Bill, applies to the court to become his guardian, and the court approves a plan for Don to live at home with care.

Don has advanced dementia and has recently developed a swallowing disorder. His doctors have prescribed a diet of thickened liquids. Bill has hired a nurse Case Manager to help him plan for Don's increasing needs. Nia has always thought of Don as a grandfather. She adores Don and his brother, who have spoiled her with special attention throughout the young woman's life. Nia dislikes the Case Manager and resents her "tone" when being told how to take care of Don. She has never noticed Don's "swallowing disorder" and she thinks the Case Manager is just trying to tell her what to do.

One night on her way home from an appointment, Nia passes Don's favorite Cantonese Chinese restaurant. She knows that by the time she gets home, Don's night caregiver will be asleep. Determined that no one denies her beloved uncle his favorite foods, Nia loads up a take-out order with barbecued ribs, chicken chow mein and shrimp with almonds, and heads home.

The Reality: Family Members Aren't Always Capable

Leo Tolstoy wrote in "Anna Karenina," "All happy families are alike; each unhappy family is unhappy in its own way." Every family has its history, dynamics and dysfunctions. If family members have not gotten along in easy times, it may be impossible in a time of stress to craft a home-based care plan requiring them to collaborate. Siblings are just people who grew up together a long time ago, and, even with some genetic material in common, they all have matured into different personalities. They may each have vastly different perceptions of their parents, their family of origin, and the home in which they were raised. When decisions about the care of an ailing senior are complicated by unresolved history between parents and children and between the children themselves, the care plan may become secondary to the family tension. Family strife may present nearly impenetrable barriers to efforts to move ahead.[14] When everyone is mired in the past, no one has the energy to look to the future.

---

[14] I had a client whose father needed care, but would only accept services from his youngest daughter. The client's rage at the way his father had overtly favored this "golden child" boiled over. While the litigation ensued, he called me daily to recount the slights he had suffered over the years; he was bitter over the fact that while his parents had encouraged him to go to technical college, his youngest sister had been sent to an Ivy League college and graduate school. The client was 75 and his sister long since retired, but a half-century later the client's anger at his parents and resentment at his sister were as sharp and bitter as ever.

Most importantly, personality clashes and family history can dominate the agenda and crowd out consideration of the senior's needs. It's not that the history is false or that the feelings aren't valid, it's just that now is not the time for that debate to be held. It always pains me when all of the sides—who are equally contributing to the failure of peacemaking—proclaim their love for and laser focus on the senior and blame the other guy for failing to win the peace.

Serving as a family caregiver can be a road to conflict with siblings who generally agree. Reasonable people may disagree with the care being provided or have a view of the senior's abilities and disabilities that is at odds with the caregiver's. Although siblings can provide vital support to one another, they can also fail entirely to provide a helping hand. Families are lifetimes of memory and experience. When siblings are facing the loss of a parent, the strains between them can become a significant source of anxiety and depression for the senior who is aware of their troubles and for the caregivers, too.[15]

A home-based plan involving an extended family cannot work unless everyone is on board. Sibling rivalry is not always left in the past, and families can be shattered by

---

[15] I have been asked how I explain the difference between family law and elder law, and here is my definition. In **family law**, the parents are divorcing each other and fighting over the children. In **elder law**, the siblings are getting divorced and they are fighting over their parents (money).

historic antagonism. I was involved once with a family of siblings, all over age 60. When we tried to mediate a care plan for their elderly ailing mother, the siblings split into what I could only imagine were historic childhood alliances—two by two—and everyone arrayed against the middle kid. In my mind's eye, I could see them as adolescents, hitting and pinching, calling names and kicking each other under the dinner table. They had all enjoyed distinguished careers and some had children and even grandchildren. But they were still mad at each other and their parent's needs gave them a space where they could finally air their grievances.

This is not meant to be judgmental; every family has issues. But, to create a workable plan to provide in-homecare, ideally the senior's whole family should be involved. This can create an opportunity for long-simmering conflicts to be aired, whether they are on topic or wildly off the subject of your ailing senior. The issues between the siblings may be submerged and erupt as disagreements about the contours of a care plan. You may not be fighting with your brother about whatever is on your mind, but at least you're venting some steam. It can be useful to have a medical professional present to weigh in on the plan that is being developed.

When one family member is designated as the chief care provider, tensions and jealousies may flare due to the perception of unequal power in the family. The caretaking child may need respite or other support while taking care of a dying parent, because managing his own emotions and the response of the ill person's surviving spouse may be overwhelming.

A comprehensive health care plan will ensure that the senior executes a Durable Health-Care Power of attorney and designates a substitute health care decision-maker, and at least one alternate. The mere act of designating one sibling over another as agent can inflame sibling dysfunction, because the agent is now in a position of power and is also in a position to collect information about the senior. Francis Bacon said "Knowledge is power," and he must have had a sibling and an ailing parent. I have seen more cases than I care to recall where one sibling used his authority to deny a sibling access to a parent and access to any information about the parent.[16]

The chosen health care fiduciary is known as a **"surrogate decision-maker."** This person "stands in the shoes" of the senior, and must, when possible, make health care decisions the senior would make if he could. If the principal cannot express his wishes, the health care surrogate must make decisions that are in the principal's objective "best interests." This is known as the "substituted judgment" standard of

---

[16] The most extreme abuses of power of attorney often involve attempts to use authority as an agent under the power of attorney to restrict the senior's right to see or talk to other people. All citizens are imbued with fundamental rights under the U.S. Constitution. One of those rights is freedom of association, and it can only be abridged by a court of law after a hearing with notice to the affected parties.

decision-making.[17] It can be a challenge to follow the dictates of a principal who is directing the decision-maker to make poor choices as a result of impaired cognition or undue influence.

The challenges to creating a sustainable care plan is a reflection of the era in which we are living. Longer life expectancies means a higher likelihood of needing a higher level of services and a greater chance you'll need institutional care. It is estimated that 84% of people born in 2010 will live to age 65 or older. Since 1985, the number of citizens aged 90 years and older has nearly tripled.[18] Medical and pharmaceutical costs are increasing faster than incomes and can pose an insurmountable burden on seniors who seem poised to have to choose between eating and taking their medications.

Single households, working women and geographic distance between families have fundamentally altered the availability of stay-at-home caregivers. Providing consistent, quality care at home may sound wonderful but it may tax family members beyond their limits. Emergencies and crises in care are more likely to occur in home-based settings, where the caregivers may lack clinical skills and overlook changes in health status that signal potential problems. The failure of monitoring

---

[17] http://medical-dictionary.thefreedictionary.com/best+interest+standard

[18] http://blog.aarp.org/2014/12/11/whats-different-about-family-caregiving-today.

and early detection has been blamed for the higher rates of emergency room and hospital services by seniors in home health settings.

If you are aware of a family "situation" and ignore this reality when you create your family-based care plan, it will blow apart, probably at a very inconvenient time. I wish I had a dollar for every time a family carefully made a plan to move a parent into care until someone balked and claimed that "moving Mom is wrong!" causing the whole clan to retreat to the first step of the family care narrative. I'd hang up the phone and wonder how long it would be until I heard from them next. Possibly the worst flaw in a family care plan is that when there's an emergency— for example, the schooled provider is ill, the failure of your plan is likely to leave you responsible for the senior's care until a new plan is in place. I don't mean to sound flippant, but why would you do this to yourself?

Tools for the Caregiver: Creating an End-of-Life Care Plan

As the senior's health deteriorates and he or she needs increasing care and support, the senior's agent, under the Durable Healthcare Power of Attorney, assumes a greater share of the senior's healthcare decision-making. This care plan includes a variety of supportive services that will enable the elder to remain safely at home through the end of life.

A care plan for a frail, failing senior focuses on daily supervision of the senior's condition including: chronic and acute medical issues, changes in health or care needs, medication management as well as the schedules and responsibilities for families, friends and caregivers.

1. Establishing a Daily Cover Plan

A home-based care plan for a frail senior should include attention to these details:

- Daily review of blood pressure, appetite, weight gain or loss, skin integrity, sleep patterns and bowel and bladder health
- Companionship; opportunities for socialization including attention to religious and spiritual needs
- Chronic and acute medical issues
- Schedules and responsibilities for family, friends and professional caregivers
- Medication management (daily administration, ordering refills, reporting side effects)

- Meal preparation and food shopping
- Bathing, dressing, hygiene, toileting
- Nursing care (wound care, injections)
- Occupational and physical therapy, and
- Housekeeping

2. Hiring a Home Health Care Service

The senior's care plan needs to be supplemented by professional care services. Hiring care for a frail senior is the fiduciary's job and he or she must ensure that help is appropriate and adequate.

When looking into a professional agency, here are questions to ask:

- Is the agency licensed by the State?
- What type of credentials does the staff have?
- Is the staff trained, bonded, etc.?
- Does the agency provide the level of assistance the senior requires?
- Does the agency provide an explanation of the senior's rights and responsibilities?
- Does the agency ensure patient confidentiality?
- Does the agency staff administer medications?
- Does the agency staff provide wound and dressing care?

- Does the agency staff provide physical, occupational or speech therapy?

a. Seeking Applicants

- Write a detailed job description that defines all the caretaking tasks involved, the hours and days of the job, and preferences with regard to driving and other transportation options.

- Decide how much you're prepared to pay. If you hire someone directly, you need to look into how you will pay taxes and possibly a Social Security contribution. Check with the Internal Revenue Service http:/www.irs.gov for proper tax forms and instructions. See the IRS publications "<u>Hiring Household Employees</u>" and "<u>Independent Contractor (Self-Employed) or Employee?</u>" for information on your obligation to report and pay taxes.

b. Conducting an Interview

- Ask job candidates to bring a résumé or job history as well as names and telephone numbers for at least two references.

- Describe to applicants the senior's needs, health concerns, likes and dislikes. Outline the duties you expect her to perform. Be friendly but professional. Limit your questions to those that will help you determine if this person is a good match for the job.

- Get the applicant's name, address, telephone number and Social Security number. Don't be afraid to ask for proof of identity, ideally a Social Security card. If not available, ask to see a driver's license or other photo ID. Do a background check before making any hires.

- Find out if the applicant has any special training, such as experience working with clients who have dementia. Also ask about work history, including why the applicant left her former job.

- Ask about the applicant's expectations of this position and why the applicant is working in the home care field.

- Invite the applicant to ask questions about the job and your expectations.

- Be clear about salary and benefits, such as vacations and other time off. Head off any misunderstandings by addressing these issues directly.

c. Checking References

- Always call the references.

- If the reference is a former employer, ask about punctuality and attendance as well as the precise nature of the work position. Find out why the applicant left the position, and whether there were any problems. Take notes on each applicant so you can refer to them when making your decision.

- Pay for a criminal background check. Contact your local law enforcement agency to find out how to do this.

- Consider hiring for a one-month trial period before you commit to a permanent hire. Explain that this would be an opportunity to see if this is a mutually acceptable arrangement.
- Once someone accepts your job offer, put the entire agreement in writing and have both of you sign and date this. Include information about the trial period, job duties, salary, pay schedule, time off, start date and termination policy. Keep copies of the job contract signed by both of you.
- Try to be at home for the first few days to familiarize the new caregiver with the routine. Periodically, drop by unannounced to check on how things are going.

d. Professional Guidance

- A professional nurse case manager (also called a "care manager") may provide important support to the family. In home-based settings, conflict between family members can flare when someone disagrees with an assessment of the senior's needs or other elements of the care plan. The care plan is about the senior's needs and not about the family, but attention may shift away from the senior when tensions flare and the family is unable to resolve differences of opinion. A care manager can be helpful in steering the conversation away from intra-family dynamics and explaining the available options to the family.

e. Respite Care
- Caregiving for anyone can be a physically challenging and emotionally draining experience, but when the patient is a beloved parent or partner, the weight of emotions can be unbearable. Caregivers may become so consumed with their tasks for the senior that they neglect to take care of themselves. Unfortunately, the emotional and physical strain of caregiving, day in and day out, can lead to stress, burnout and even physical illness.
- Professional or family members can provide care so that the primary care to her can have regular time off. Hiring a professional case manager can provide the family with access to additional resources including respite caregivers who can step in on a periodic basis to relieve the primary caregiver or to support or even replace that caregiver when the care needs become too heavy.

Myth #4: When I Can No Longer Manage My Money and Financial Affairs, A Trusted Person Will Handle My Finances.

The same forces that lead seniors to deny a need for personal care unite to keep them from proactively creating a plan for the management of their money and property. Today's seniors did not grow up in our "Oprah" style confessional culture. Finances and income are private matters, not to be discussed, especially not with children.[19] Many seniors regard financial and estate planning with suspicion and regard all of it as unwelcome, complicated and managed by unscrupulous hucksters. These are the so-called "Depression-Era Babies," who as children witnessed their parents lose their homes and saw the nation's financial institutions and financiers come tumbling down. When the stock market crashed in 1929, some 15–25 million Americans owned stocks or had family members who did.[20] Many seniors are afraid of the cost involved in planning. They aren't familiar with lawyers or how they work and they are afraid of getting caught up in a process with an unknown cost.

---

[19] https://bucks.blogs.nytimes.com/2010/11/09/talking-with-depression-era-parents-about-money

[20] ps://realtruth.org/articles/090105-003-anal

As every procrastinator knows, timing is everything. When a senior falls ill, is injured, or suddenly displays a noticeable change in thinking or behavior, it may be too late for him to do any planning at all. If the necessary documentation is not in place, no one will have the authority needed to make important decisions and no one will be designated to have access to important information.

When the senior no longer has the necessary "transactional capacity" to sign a power of attorney, it's too late to find a "less restrictive alternative" to a court-supervised guardianship. If the senior hasn't yet made decisions about who will be the financial decision-maker, there may be no option other than to seek a guardianship.

The loss of cognition isn't akin to the difference between dark and light. The disease process is slow and may not manifest itself immediately in ways that are noticeable. It's not uncommon for a family to be unaware that a senior is forgetting to pay the bills until they arrive at the home and there is no electricity. As with all other signs of diminishing cognition, the senior often is unaware that he's not managing. I've had any number of seniors proudly display check registers that showed no recent entries with no numbers that bore any resemblance to checks recently written.

The same diseases that strip the brain's ability to read and write may also interfere with a senior's ability to read social cues and exercise judgment in the choice of friends. Some seniors who may be experiencing paranoia or anxiety can be influenced to reject a trusted relative and become attached to a "new best friend" who ultimately betrays the senior's trust.

Is Your Plan Safe?

- Mary, 84, is a recent widow. One afternoon, she gets a knock on the door. A young man presents his business card. He is a door-to-door stockbroker. The widow is charmed by his suit, tie and good looks. She has been dreadfully lonely lately and she invites the young man inside for a cup of tea. He leaves a business card and a brochure with flyers discussing investment models. The widow sets them aside; the graphs are confusing and the text is so small she can't read it anyway. The young stockbroker reappears the next afternoon bearing a bouquet of flowers. The widow is thrilled at the thought of another afternoon chat. On the third day, he appears with a bottle of wine and a young woman he introduces as his fiancée. The young couple talk excitedly about their impending marriage. Has she read the materials he left, asks the stockbroker? "Oh yes", replies the widow. When he leaves he is holding a signed check in his name for $350,000.

  The bank contacts Mary a few days later. The check has bounced. Mary is mortified, but she cannot recall the name of the investment broker nor does she recall writing the check.

Is Your Plan Sustainable?

- Myra, 80, is recently widowed and doesn't want to live alone. She asks her daughter, Sue, if she would think about moving in to help her. Sue has been married and divorced several times. She is retired, but always short on cash. Sue offers to help Myra balance her checkbook and manage the bills. Since Myra's husband always did these tasks, Myra is relieved to have Sue's help. In Sue's free time, she decides to learn about short selling stocks on the Internet. She sets up an Internet business buying organic garden seeds and reselling these online. Sue's income is strained so she covers her excess spending with Myra's cash account. She accepts a few new credit cards that come in the mail to help manage the household expenses.

Myra's son, Ed, is a co-signer on her bank account and receives duplicate copies of her credit card statements. After a few months, he starts tracking the credit card charges and calculates that Sue is spending about $10,000 each month on her business ventures. When Ed tries to discuss this situation with Sue, she screams at him and hangs up the phone. Within an hour, Ed and the rest of the family receive a shrill email from Sue discussing the sacrifices she has made for Myra and explaining that Myra has agreed in private conversation that Sue may use her funds as she wishes. She also states that Myra is disappointed and upset that only Sue—alone among the family—appears to love Myra. Sue is certainly the only child, she says, who has demonstrated her devotion to their mother.

Sue explains that Ed's accusations have upset Myra terribly and that she does not wish to speak to anyone in the family. When Ed tries to call Myra, he gets her voice message. From then on, Sue acts as the "gatekeeper" for Myra and the family has fewer and fewer opportunities to visit with her. Sue will not allow anyone to visit with Myra unless she is present. The family is upset that Sue is limiting access to Myra but have no idea what to do.

Will You be Targeted for Exploitation?

- Ethel is 90. She has survived two husbands and is quite a wealthy widow. She lives in a beautiful home with a sweeping view of the mountains and sea to the west. She has a daughter, Ella, with whom she has always been close. Ethel also survived cancer and refuses to go the doctor anymore. This has become a source of conflict with Ella. More and more, their conversations end with Ethel sounding irritable.

Ethel has always taken in strays. Lately these include a man named Tony. Ethel explains to Ella that Tony is staying with Ethel in exchange for caretaking services around the house. Tony's girlfriend, Ann, has been staying over lately, too. When Ella comes to visit, she notices a new TV in the living room. She begins to see packages arriving that disappear into Tony and Ann's room.

Ella is the agent under Ethel's financial and health care power of attorney and she begins to worry. Ella and Ethel quarrel one day after Ethel fails to attend a medical appointment. When she calls the next day, Tony answers and says Ethel does not want to speak to her. Ella doesn't hear from Ethel for a few days, but she is busy with work and her kids. She finally drives over to Ethel's home on Saturday and finds that her house key doesn't fit the lock. Ann answers the door and explains that Ethel does not want to see her. She goes into the house and returns with fresh copies of powers of attorney appointing Tony and Ann as Ethel's agent.

There are websites devoted to the Top 10 Senior Frauds (and seemingly no end to the inventiveness of the criminal mind). Ironically, Internet scams directed at seniors are their own species of fraud and have spawned hundreds of progeny, stealing money as they grow. There is also an unintended consequence created from Internet dating that has created an especially insidious species of danger.

- Sarah is 79 and lives in her home with her youngest daughter, Emily, 45, who never married. Sarah has insulin-dependent diabetes and related complications—she is legally blind and has neuropathy in her feet. Emily provides vital care, pays the bills and manages Sarah's income. She takes Sarah to all her appointments, and cares for the home.

  Emily met a man, Jeff, on the Internet a few months ago. She is smitten. Jeff is 50 and works as a handyman around town. Jeff and Emily are talking about getting married and have approached Sarah about using her home as collateral to purchase a larger property where they could live and manage as a Bed & Breakfast. Jeff has his eye on a great property and says he would do all the work on the project to save money. He just needs Sarah to provide the down payment.

One day Emily brings an envelope of papers to Sarah and asks her to sign them. Emily explains that Jeff has approached a banker to acquire a mortgage and they want $250,000. Sarah has always been frugal and paid off her mortgage years ago. She is reluctant to sign, but Emily gets angry. The younger woman cautions that unless Sarah signs the paperwork, Jeff will leave her. And, Emily threatens, if Jeff leaves, she is going with him.

Sarah is caught between her concern about her finances and her daughter's connection with Jeff. She feels she has no choice, so she signs the paperwork.

The Reality: Seniors are Uniquely Vulnerable.

The ripping off of America's senior citizens has become an industry costing America's elderly nearly $36 billion annually in lost resources.[21] There are several main types of financial abuse: theft, fraud and exploitation.

Frauds targeting seniors include fake credit card schemes, lottery and prize promotions, phony investment sales and "sweetheart scams." The people who commit fraud are typically strangers and opportunists. The term **"exploitation"** refers to the use of the senior's money and assets by another person for that person's benefit. It is more common for those engaged in financial exploitation of seniors to be that person's family member, a friend and/or a caregiver.

Research shows that as the human brain ages, the pathways that receive, process and transmit information weaken.[22]

---

[21] http://www.cambiahealth.com

[22] Nathan Spreng, director of Cornell University Laboratory of Brain and Cognition, has reported that behavioral testing and MRI scans reveal that the brains of seniors who had been exploited showed more shrinkage and less connectivity in two key areas than those of seniors who had not been victimized. The study found the affected brains did not signal the senior when he was faced with risky situations. The study also found that the area of the brain that helps read social cues showed more shrinkage and fewer neural connections. Researchers found that the networks of the affected brain regions were interconnected, and that the combination of effects might leave those seniors affected by these brain changes more vulnerable to scams. http://www.cbsnews.com/news/seniors-brain-changes-could-make-them-vulnerable-to-scams

As a result, it takes older adults longer to learn and process new information. All of us are able to pick and choose the messages we prefer to hear, and this tendency becomes more marked over time, so that as we get older we increasingly filter out the negative messages in favor of the positive. Along with the loneliness that comes with illness, incapacity and social isolation, the changes in cognition increase a senior's vulnerability to deception and fraud. The shut-in senior won't hear the wheedling or bullying tone in a telemarketer's calls as clearly as he will understand that he's lonely and that his son is too busy. The senior will focus on the daily calls of the nice young man who asks about his health, and then asks him for money for some cause or to secure a prize.

Senior abuse, like spousal abuse, lives in the shadows. Some victims do not report abuse because they are afraid of retaliation. If the abuser is also the senior's caregiver, revealing their financial crimes might result in the loss of the caregiver, causing the senior's dream of living and dying at home to come crashing down. The senior may fear that without the caregiver he will be put in an institution.

Ninety percent of the abusers of senior citizens are their family members. 50% percent of the abusers are adult children and 20% are partners or spouses.

Their frailty appears to increase their vulnerability to becoming crime statistics. In one report, victims aged 65 and older were much more likely than younger victims to be killed by family members for financial gain.

We all trust that we will be safe in the company and care of our family and friends, but all too often the lines blur between the person needing care, his finances and the person providing care. Family members—sons, daughters, grandchildren, spouses—may have burdens of their own that make them resentful or determined to exact some form of compensation from the senior—or from the senior's family—for their efforts. These individuals may have long-standing feelings toward the senior or other family members. They may feel entitled to take from the senior before his savings are depleted and he dies; they may want to take their "share" before other family members get a portion of the inheritance. As the senior declines and stops overseeing his own finances, the caregiver's feelings of entitlement, anger and resentment may lead him to abuse the trust of the senior through acts of financial exploitation and abuse. There may be a million justifications, but this conduct is illegal.

- John, 92, has late-stage ALS. He owns a small home on waterfront property. The land has lately skyrocketed in value. John has twin sons, Pete and Paul. Paul lives in John's spare room and has taken care of him for years while also working. Paul is John's agent under powers of attorney. Pete stops by when he can, but he is busy with his life, which includes a wife with terminal cancer. As John is failing, Paul begins to feel more and more stressed and begins to believe that Pete is not entitled to share in their father's estate because he cannot be a caretaker. Paul goes on line and does some reading and writes up a deed that transfers John's property to himself. John trusts Paul and when Paul tells his father that transferring the land now will save money, John signs the deed placed in front of him.[23]

Generally, vulnerable adults are defined as persons who lack the ability to independently manage all of the activities of daily living and are dependent on others for assistance. The dependent seniors may be developmentally delayed, subject to a court-created guardianship or receiving care services at home or in a care community.

---

[23] If you have been in a close and confidential relationship to a person during life and they have made you gifts, a legal presumption is made that those gifts were obtained by undue influence. If a party contests the lifetime gifts, the burden of proof shifts to the gift recipient to prove that the gifts were free and volitional and that they were not the product of undue influence.

Tools for the Caregiver: What to Do if a Senior Has Been Financially Exploited.

First, if you believe there is any imminent threat of *physical harm* to the senior, call 9-1-1.

Financial Exploitation.

If you believe that *financial exploitation* is ongoing, try to speak about your concerns to the senior. If you are not able to persuade the senior that a problem exists or that a change is needed, you will need to pursue resolution through the courts. At this time, the states still retain a patchwork of laws regarding adult guardianships and protective laws regarding vulnerable adults—although a uniform, national law regarding vulnerable adults has been proposed. Most states have laws permitting seniors or persons acting on the senior's behalf to seek a temporary restraining order or a temporary guardianship on behalf of a senior who is being financially exploited.

Court Orders under Power of Attorney.

If a principal suffering from impaired judgment is at financial risk as a result of the improper influence of a third party, the agent must act to protect the principal. An agent may not stand silent while another person commits a fraud against the principal.

Generally, when a principal vetoes a proposal by the agent, the agent cannot act. In many states, an agent under power of attorney may petition the court for an order that authorizes the agent to overrule the principal's veto and act.

- As an example, say you need to secure a reverse mortgage on your mother's home to help pay for her care. She has no other options and she doesn't understand how the mortgage works. You can present the facts to the court and ask a judge to approve this plan and issue an order authorizing you to enter into the mortgage on her behalf.

- Your daughter is a heroin addict, but your mother has a soft spot for the girl and regularly gifts her money that she uses to buy drugs. Your mother doesn't understand that she is literally feeding your daughter's habit. You are your mother's agent and you want her to stop giving away her money like this, but you **may not** tell your mother that she cannot gift money to her granddaughter. However, you **may** ask a court to order that reasonable limitations be placed on your mother's unfettered right to make these gifts.

Action for the Protection of a Vulnerable Adult.

It may be necessary to begin a court action for the protection of a vulnerable person and seek temporary restraining orders against a third party you suspect of financial abuse or exploitation. All 50 states and the District of Columbia have enacted legislation to protect the rights of vulnerable seniors. Some seniors are groomed to trust their abusers and eventually ally with the people who are victimizing them. This behavior is called the "Stockholm Syndrome," and it is characterized by hostages who grow sympathetic toward their captors.[7] If this is the case with your senior, and you are a named a fiduciary, you may have to bring an action for the protection of a person who doesn't see the need for protection at all and may side against you in court.

Generally, actions for the protection of a vulnerable adult will err on the side of protecting the senior, and will, on a temporary basis, restrain an alleged perpetrator from continuing to commit acts of abuse, abandonment, fraud or exploitation. The temporary restraints are then subject to a further court hearing and determination of the existence of a threat to the senior. In these protective actions, the court can order a third party suspected of abuse to stay away from the senior, refrain from spending or using property, or produce an accounting of the senior's funds.

Once **Temporary Restraining Orders** are issued, the defendant has a chance to appear and defend himself against the claims made. After a hearing, the court may keep the restraints in place or cancel them; the court may require additional materials to be brought before the court for review, and may appoint an attorney or guardian *ad litem* for the senior. A guardian *ad litem* can be appointed to act in a lawsuit or on behalf of a child, elderly parent or other person who is not considered capable of representing themselves.

- You are an agent for your long-married aunt and uncle. They own everything 50/50. One day, you are at their home when a bank representative calls to ask about the large withdrawals made by your aunt. It turns out that she has been visiting the bank regularly with a young man, giving lavish cash gifts to her "new friend." As an agent for both spouses, you have to act to restrain your aunt who is being exploited and who is giving away assets that also belong to your uncle, to whom you owe a separate and equal duty.

- Your mother has dementia and her eyesight is failing. She has lately become angry at what she calls your "interference" in her affairs. You suspect she is afraid because she knows she is losing her vision and will become more dependent on you as time moves on. Instead of your help, she has now put her trust in the neighbor's son, Bob, who seems to be at the house all day and night. One day, the checkbook is sitting open at your mother's house and you stop and take a look. You see that Bob has been writing the checks, and you notice he has written several large checks to himself.

A petition for orders of protection for a vulnerable adult may be filed, along with a petition to establish a guardianship for an incapacitated senior who has become a target of financial exploitation or abuse. While an action for protection of a vulnerable adult addresses a specific actor and a specific set of circumstances, a guardianship is more wide-ranging in nature and is intended to be a permanent solution.[20] The facts asserted in the vulnerable adult protective action may serve as the basis of the petition to establish a guardianship.

Guardianship.

You have a power of attorney but the senior/principal has taken action to nullify it (stating, "You're fired," cancels the power of attorney). If you believe this senior is at risk as to her personal affairs or money and property, you can file a petition with a court to commence a **guardianship** (also called a **conservatorship**) of that senior.

A **guardianship** creates a system of a court-supervised program of assistance for individuals who are "at risk" as a result of a "demonstrated inability over time" to perform necessary tasks. Having a guardian doesn't mean you will be forced into a nursing home. It does mean that a court will be asked to review a proposed budget and a plan of personal care developed by your guardian. For example, a senior wants to live at home, although he can't afford to pay for in-home care and the house is falling down around his ears. The guardian *can't* force the senior to move, but he *can* ask the court to order that the house be sold. The senior cannot be forced to relocate, but realistically, he won't have any place to live after the new buyer tears down the house to rebuild.

In making the decision to move forward with a guardianship, you are drawing a line in the sand between the capacitated past and the future. When seniors have some residual capacity they can rail against being dubbed "incapacitated" and they may rage against the child who has had the temerity to actually begin this process. A guardianship may generally be filed by any person who has a credible belief that another person is at risk to his person or estate.

After the guardianship petition is filed, the court appoints an investigator, often called a **"guardian ad litem"** to review the substance of the petition for guardianship, meet with the alleged incapacitated person and others, and answer three questions: (1) is a guardianship needed? (2) are there any less restrictive alternatives that might be created instead of a guardianship (such as trusts or powers of attorney); and (3) if a guardian is needed, who should it be and what powers should the guardian have?

In a guardianship action, it is critically important to make sure that the person who is the subject of the petition receives notice of the petition. The alleged incapacitated person will have the right to have the court appoint an attorney, and also has the right to a trial on the issue of whether or not he is "incapacitated." In most states, mediation has replaced the courtroom as the preferred place to negotiate the terms of a guardianship with the incapacitated person and family members.

The court will seek a medical report on the status of the alleged incapacitated person and will rely on the report and recommendations of the investigator as to who should be appointed as guardian and as to the scope of the guardian's duties. The alleged incapacitated person, the petitioner, and other family members can weigh in as to their preferences for guardian. Family members can seek to be appointed as guardian, and there is a preference for family to serve when this is possible. In cases where there is tension between the family over the senior's care or the senior's estate, however, the court will tend *not* to appoint a family member.

The court usually requires that the guardian make an annual report to the court regarding the ward's affairs. A guardianship is terminated when the ward recovers his capacity or dies.

Powers of Attorney: Uses and Abuses

A financial (sometimes "general") power of attorney allows an agent to "stand in the shoes of the principal" and exercise her rights with regard to money and property in making healthcare decisions. An agent is expected to consult with the principal and follow her expressed desires. If communication isn't possible, the agent should look at the principal's historic actions for guidance with regard to things like investment styles, risk tolerances and decisions involving heath care treatment. This is called **substituted judgment**. Put simply, the principal should make decisions on the basis of what the principal could do/would do if she were able to act. Where there is no guidance, and even when applying substituted judgment, an agent must act in the best interests of the principal. This is called **the best interests** standard of decision-making.

As a fiduciary, a financial agent's duties include:

Accounting to the principal

Acting at all times with utmost loyalty to the principal, the agent must avoid misusing the trusted relationship by profiting from it financially. A power of attorney has been called the "keys to the castle," because the agent has the authority to act without control, and if the principal is not available to supervise him, there may be no one to ensure that the agent is doing her duty, such as keeping an accounting of the principal's income and disbursements.[24]

If an agent will be compensated by the principal for services, this agreement should be prepared or at least reviewed by an attorney who solely represents the senior. If the agent writes a contract for an incapacitated principal and sets his own terms and then signs the contract on behalf of the unknowing principal, this is a breach of the (1) duty of loyalty; (2) duty to account; (3) duty to avoid conflicts of interest and (4) duty to avoid earning a profit from the existence of a confidential relationship.

---

[24] An "accounting" is ill-defined at law, but at the very least the financial agent should maintain an up-to-date record of income and spending (what, when, where, and cost) and keep receipts for expenditures. This verification is critical in preparing annual individual income tax returns, which is another fiduciary obligation. If anyone accuses the agent of misusing the principal's funds, records are vital.

Families often lend money, share living spaces and rely on each other for help of all kinds. That's what families are for. But in some cases, this kind of close-knit family interaction can lead to claimed—and actual—financial abuse and exploitation involving the family member/agent. It is important to note that a gift, payment for services or any other exchange of value between an agent and principal during the principal's lifetime is presumed, at law, to have come about the through the agent's exercise of **undue influence**. For example, a terminally ill senior/principal gifts his home to his son, who has been living at home and providing his care. After the father's death, his daughters file a lawsuit against the son and assert that the brother, as agent, exercised undue influence over the principal while he was a **vulnerable adult**. In court, the son now has the **burden of proof** to show that the father's gift was made freely and knowingly.

The presumption does not apply to gifts made in wills or testamentary trusts (effective only at death).

Myth #5: I Don't Want To Do Any Estate Planning And I Don't Need A Will. When I Die, My Family Will Sort It Out.

Every state has a law setting out a plan for the distribution of the estate of a person who dies without leaving a will ("intestate"). In my years as an attorney, I've always been surprised at how many financially successful and commercially savvy people don't have a simple will or powers of attorney. It's become fashionable to be wary of the government. It always surprises me then that people won't do their estate planning. The reality is that if you do not create a will or a trust to manage your estate after your life ends, you are leaving very personal decisions—who will inherit your estate and who will administer your estate—to the determination of your state's legislators.

Many years ago, when I was still answering my own phone and typing all of my own documents, a prospective client called. He wanted to know what I would charge him to write a will. I charged $80/hour in those days, so I told him the cost would be $300.

"Three hundred dollars? I'm not paying you $300 for a will! That's robbery! I could go and print a will off the

Internet right now. For free! Why do I need you at all?" he roared in my ear.

I was stumped. The caller was correct—there were all sorts of legal forms on the Internet that he could download and use at no cost.

"You're right," I said to the caller.

"Right? What do you mean?" he shouted back.

"Well," I said, "think of it this way. If you make your own will and the distribution provisions don't work or the will is not valid, you'll be dead, so you won't know. Right? It may be a huge mess for your family, but it won't be an issue for you at all."

You're gambling with your life savings.

- Dora is 88, hale and hearty. She has three children. Her eldest son, Mark, is the apple of her eye. Her daughters dote on their mother and provide the care and assistance that allows her to live, as she insists, in her own home.

  Dora sews her own clothes, keeps a chicken in the yard for eggs and cans her garden vegetables. She doesn't see the need for a doctor, a lawyer or an accountant. She remembers a simpler time when people made agreements with each other on the basis of a handshake, and paid each other with a day's labor. Now, she's a dinosaur because she wants to pay her bills with a check and talk to customer assistance on the phone instead of typing on a computer.

She keeps her money in a bank account; Mark's name is also on the account so that he can pay her bills. Dora has a will, made years ago, that names Mark to receive her entire estate. This is a mistake: Dora has always told her children that when she dies they are to share her estate in thirds. But she puts off going to see a lawyer to rewrite the will because she is afraid of what it will cost. "Don't worry about my estate," Dora has said to her daughters so often they know her words by heart, "when I die, Mark will do what is right."

Dora dies in her sleep one night. Mark is appointed as the estate executor. In order to inherit from Dora, Mark must survive her by 30 days, a standard "survivorship" clause. On the 31st day after Dora dies, Mark has a heart attack and dies. Dora's estate is now part of Mark's estate, which goes to Mark's widow.

Dora's daughter's try to contact Mark's widow. They receive a letter from an attorney stating that she will sue them for harassment if they attempt to contact her again.

I often think that fear is underpinning the decision not to move ahead—fear of change, fear of the unknown, fear of committing to a course of action. It is particularly difficult to create an estate plan when family members are in conflict and the estate plan might be seen as a surrogate for a parent's approval. Just as they jockeyed for attention when they were younger, they want to be recognized as the most reliable child with the best judgment.

It's important to remember that there is no law that says you must leave your estate in equal shares or even that it must be equitable. As long as you have legal capacity, as that is defined, you can make or change your will or trust. Importantly, the fact that you are subject to a guardianship does not necessarily mean that you lack capacity; under certain circumstances even people with diagnosed dementia are able to make changes to these documents. to make or change a Will.[25]

Creating a will requires that parents address some uncomfortable realities about their children. Just as most parents view the success of their children as a mirror of their successful parenting, a child who has never left the nest speaks to our failures. More than one adult child has taken financial support from parents over a lifetime. In settling an estate plan, parents must decide whether or not to call out money that was loaned or gifted in the

---

[25] "Legal capacity" means that you have the proper state of mind to make a till or trust. In law school, they called it a "three-legged stool" because capacity has three elements: (1) You must know the natural objects of your affection; (2) you must understand the nature and extent of your estate, (3) and you must be free from undue influence, coercion or duress.

past and address whether or not it will be paid back at a future date. Gifts or financial aid to one child over an extended period will reduce an estate, so in reality this one sibling will have taken a larger share of the estate than the others. It's easier not to act than to commit to this in writing, especially knowing you won't be there to help the family deal with the decisions you have made.

You Aren't Doing Your Family Any Favors.

- Joan, 68, inherited the home in which she and her husband, Al, have lived and raised their family. Joan has end-stage lung cancer. She is withering away from the disease and her lack of appetite. She can't sleep at night, and when the house is quiet she soothes her anxieties with online auctions. Box after unopened box of goods are stacked in an extra bedroom, which is becoming impassable.

  Al retired a few years ago when Joan got too ill to do any work around the house. He loves their home, and his passion for gardening has turned the yard into parkland. Over the years, Al used his talents as an architect and handyman to improve the house, and he has it set up now as the perfect, peaceful spot for his retirement.

  Joan and Al have a son, Max. Max and Al used to be best friends, but Max has made lifestyle choices Al doesn't agree with, and they are barely speaking to each other. Every time Max and Al meet lately, a fight erupts. Max lives in a mobile home at the back of their land, a long-term situation that isn't working so well anymore. Max used to pay rent, then he lost his job and started helping Al with the yard and housework instead of paying rent. For the last few months, Max has been unemployed and hasn't paid rent or done any work. He hangs around his home during the day as a stream of friends go in and out. Al dislikes Max's friends and fears they are drug dealers. He especially dislikes Max's live-in girlfriend and her rowdy kids.

Over the years, Joan has heard that it would be a simple matter to put Al's name on the title to the house, but she could never bring herself to do this. She grew up in this home, and her heart is here. Joan never worked outside the home and she has no retirement income or savings. In her mind, owning the house puts her on an equal economic footing with Al.

Joan dies without a will and the house is her separate property. Under state law, her interest in separate property goes equally to her husband and her son. As Al begins his new life as a widower and a new retiree, he finds that he owns his home with his son.

You're Giving Up Control

By preparing an estate plan, including powers of attorney and a will or living trust, you create a plan to distribute your assets that satisfies your personal goals, not the state's idea of who should get what. A **living trust** is a legal document placing assets into a trust (of investments), for example. At death, they are transferred to the beneficiaries by a chosen representative.

A **living will** or advance directive or advance healthcare directive is a written statement outlining wishes regarding medical treatment when a person is no longer able to express his or her informed consent.

By exercising your right to create a will that can be administered without Court supervision, your heirs can save time and money.

- Annette, 83, is a widow. She has outlived her whole family except her son, Bob, who rents an apartment nearby. Bob has never married, but he is the father of two toddlers, ages 2 and 4, from two different mothers. Annette is not sure she approves of Bob's lifestyle, but she adores her grandchildren. Bob has tried to talk to Annette about putting a will together, especially since he now has children, but since the death of Annette's husband, she is unwilling to discuss aging, illness, death or her thoughts on these topics.

  Annette and Bob are sports fans and they make plans to take a weekend road trip to see their favorite football team. On the way to the game, they are both killed in an automobile accident.

Bob's apartment rent goes unpaid, and finally his landlord moves to evict him. Upon learning that Bob is deceased, the judge hearing the eviction appoints an attorney in the courtroom to open probate of his estate. The administrator then learns of Annette's death and her estate is opened as well.

The heir to Annette's state is Bob; the heirs to Bob's estate are children under the age of 18. Court rules require that an underage child has a guardian *ad litem* to oversee their interest in the estates. One of Bob's children has special needs, so the court appoints a separate guardian *ad litem* for each child.

During the estate administration of Annette's estate, her house is sold. She has no Will directing her executor to act without court supervision, and the court has the interests of the minors at hand. The sale process requires a series of court hearings at which the administrator and guardians *ad litem* must each appear.

Bob's estate is worth less, but it costs more to administer. Bob was an antique car enthusiast and had parked several vehicles in varying stages of repair in local garages. The estate administrator needs to get a court order to get into each vehicle. One car needs to be rekeyed, another needs to be towed away as junk. Each automobile then needs additional authorization to be valued and sold. In the case of some autos, the cost of the legal work exceeds the value of the car.

The estates are liquidated and trusts are created to hold the funds for the children, minus the court costs and the fees of the attorneys who were assigned to the case. Going forward, the trusts created for the children will be administered by a professional trustee and will be subject to annual reviews by the court.

The Reality: Creating a Will or a Trust is a Gift to your Family

Years ago, I dated a man who worked for a national magazine publisher. His job was to formulate the glues that hold the magazine subscription cards in the seam of the journal until it's opened. The glue, if it has worked properly, has disintegrated by the time you open the magazine and the spine releases the subscription cards that fall at your feet. It seems to me that our parents act as the glue holding together even the most troubled families. Once parents are gone, the siblings are without a referee and can slip back into old ways of relating to each other.

Many seniors approach preparing a will or trust with the same enthusiasm as they would embark upon a tooth extraction without anaesthesia. They don't see the need to use their money on a lawyer for services they think are unnecessary. "I live in a community property state," someone will say. "Why do I need a will?"[26] They fear they will lose control of their assets. And I suspect there may be just a little superstition at play -- is signing a will evidence that you're preparing to die? (The answer is: NO.)

These are the basics: Any person over the age of 18 with property needs a will in order to decide who will be the estate's executor ("personal representative") and to decide who will get what. I recommend using percentages rather

---

[26] One exasperated senior said to me, "I've never been in a court in my life. I am not going there when I am dead."

than specific dollar amounts to represent the "slice" of your estate pie that will go to each of your heirs (for example, "10% of my estate to Stevie Wonder"). If you want to leave money to a person under age 18, you should direct the creation of a custodial account or a trust. You should name a trustee and at least one alternate trustee in case the primary-named person isn't available.

Burial directions do not belong in a will. Sometimes a will cannot be located for a long time after death. Burial directives can be prepared to reflect end-of-life decisions, organ donations and burial specifications.

A properly prepared will should contain language waiving the need for the executor to post a fiduciary bond, and allow the executor the maximum discretion allowed by state law to act without court intervention.

If you do not create a will, your estate will be distributed to the people deemed by the state to be your heirs, in the proportion assigned to them by state law. When there is no direction as to who will administer the estate, long-buried contests for control between family may be awakened. Knowledge is power, and in some families, controlling or releasing facts about an estate turns what should be a transparent process into a protracted battle. The cost of administering an estate that must be supervised by the court rises dramatically as a result of attorney's fees and costs. These eat away at each person's share of the estate.

This is not to say that all will be rosy if you do leave a will. There are cases where the selection of one child over another results in the unleashing of long-buried resentments. The newspapers are filled with horror stories of siblings stealing from each other in the name of estate management. Sometimes old resentments reawaken and invigorate a power struggle that costs everyone a fortune and destroys the family. Everyone knows a probate story that ended with the heirs getting nothing.[27]

Still, creating an estate plan is usually straightforward and relatively inexpensive while failing to make these decisions and commit them to writing can be unduly expensive. Make the will or create the trust document. It's a sensible, low-cost proactive step that will benefit your family. Once you've surmounted the hurdle of putting a will together, you can discuss it with your family. Perhaps you will hear a grievance that you can address by a lifetime gift or by some other means; you can also change your will during your life, as long as you have testamentary capacity (the legal and mental ability to make or alter a valid will). If you feel that the language of a will doesn't speak to the things you want to say to your loved ones, make an ethical will that will pass family values, (instead of *valuables*), to the next generation. This can be done by leaving a recorded message or by writing a family history.

---

[27] Every probate attorney has been lectured about Charles Dickens' Bleak House. That novel examines the case of *Jarndyce v. Jarndyce*, where multiple wills throw an estate into chaos. Over many twists and turns, the rightful heirs are ascertained, only to learn that the legal expenses have entirely consumed the estate.

Over many years, I have never had a client sign a will and leave the conference room disgruntled. Rather, after the will signing is complete and the elements of a plan are in place, I usually hear something like, "Wow! That was easy. I wonder why it took me so long?"

Tools for the Caregiver: Capacity to make a Will or Trust

Dying without a Will.

Here are some of the problems created by the senior who failed to leave a Will (or Trust).

- *Loss of control over who administers the estate.*

    The estate of the senior who died will be deemed **intestate** if he did not have a Will. The probate laws of the state where he died will impose certain requirements upon the person who ultimately steps forward to serve as the estate's administrator. Some states require the administrator to qualify for and post a fiduciary bond as insurance to protect the beneficiaries, heirs and creditors. This will be an extra expense to the estate. In some states, money set aside for minors requires the appointment of a special guardian *ad litem* to make sure the heirs get everything to which they are entitled and to advise the court on how to hold the money until the heirs reach maturity. If court supervision is required, that means an attorney's services are needed and the administrator will need court authority to act. Court supervision will increase the cost of administration and reduce the amount left for your heirs.

- *Loss of control over the process.*

    If the senior does not choose a personal representative prior to his death, literally anyone can approach the court and ask to be appointed as the administrator of his estate. In some states, the administrator will be required to get a court order to sell and distribute assets.

- *Loss of the opportunity to do tax planning.*

    The federal Estate Tax Exemption amount is currently $11.4 million. Some states impose inheritance taxes on an estate at a lesser value. If you do not prepare a Will or a Trust and you have a larger estate, you may fail to take advantage of tax planning that could reduce your family's future tax liability and preserve a larger share of your estate for their use.

- *Loss of control to designate who gets what.*

    Without a Will, the senior is unable to include or exclude beneficiaries, and could not direct specific assets to designated individuals. The state's law of **"descent and distribution"** determines the **"degree of kinship"** of the senior's survivors and establishes the right to inherit. Individuals in relationships not recognized by the laws of heirship—friends, unmarried partners, stepchildren—will not be in line to benefit[28]. Every person has the right to designate individuals to receive personal tangible property of an estate. This opportunity is lost when no Will or Trust exists.

- *This void can create the opportunity for family conflict to flourish*

If the deceased senior had loaned money to a person and that transaction was not documented, his estate will not likely recover these funds. This could create or exacerbate tensions within the family of that senior if he had helped a family member over the years with loans or gifts. If any of those loans or gifts were not documented, those transactions often morph into family battles after the death of the parents which could end up in the courts.

---

[28] Estates include "probate" assets that pass through a will and "non-probate" assets, like insurance policies and annuities that pass according to a beneficiary designation. If there is no beneficiary designation to a non-probate asset, it is generally distributed by intestate succession. 401(k) plans are controlled by state law, but most retirement plan accounts, pensions, IRAs, however, are controlled by the federal Employee Retirement Income Security Act of 1974 (ERISA) (Pub.L. 93–406, 88 Stat. 829, enacted September 2, 1974, codified in part at 29 U.S.C. ch. 18). Under ERISA, if the owner of a covered retirement account is married when he dies, the surviving spouse is entitled to receive 50 percent of the account, regardless of any contrary beneficiary designation, unless a Spousal Waiver has been signed. If a non-spouse is the designated beneficiary and there is no Spousal Waiver, the designated beneficiary will receive the remaining 50 percent of the account. http://www.401khelpcenter.com/401k_education/connor_beneficiary_designations.html

Conclusion

It is a fact that people of all ages subscribe to myths that help them cope with uncertainties and disappointments of life. A few examples of such myths for people at various stages of life are:

Children: The tooth-fairy and Santa Claus

Young adults: The perfect marriage and a rose-encircled cottage

Older adults: The perfect job and retirement spent vacationing in far-away places

We have dealt in this book with five myths that seniors embrace. There is a large difference between those senior myths and the others listed above to which younger people cling. When those younger people come to believe their myths and try to live by them, the results are not injurious to them even if they feel some disappointment with the reality.

This is not the case with the senior myths with which we have dealt in this book. The reason for this is that the senior is usually incapable of accepting the reality. He is frozen into inaction to make intelligent decisions because of the myths he believes. The result is that the senior is left to face physical, medical, emotional, social, legal and financial outcomes that are frequently injurious and even ruinous.

The picture we paint is not totally bleak, however. The inabilities of the senior can be largely offset if there is a caregiver who can inform himself of the options available and take actions that are appropriate, responsible and legal to fill the gap left by the senior. If this sounds like a barely adequate solution to the senior's problem, we should note that any level of improvement seems worth making the effort. Leaving seniors and their families to fail without significant help strikes us as an unacceptable alternative. We hope that the present terrible reality many seniors face will serve as a wake-up call to potential caregivers and to the various professional senior care entities. They can be of tremendous help to the senior who is struggling with his reality.

In Memoriam

<u>Affirmation</u>
<u>by Steve Adler</u>
<u>February 2019</u>

Last year, I had a melanoma on my left arm excised. That tumor was an unwelcome guest rudely thrown out of my bodily space. Now I find that the melanoma has made a seeming reappearance – a large and rapidly growing lymph node, possibly even two or more, rapidly growing nodules in my lungs, and a new lump on the same arm where the trouble had all begun. After the doctors have laid out the medical tests and likely interventions, the big unknown of what it all portends for me remains a giant question mark. These are the new and equally unwelcome guests I am left with whom to deal.

Each night as I lie down to sleep, the fluid that has accumulated and wrapped itself around my lungs has to reposition itself, and for several minutes I experience the pulmonary distress that, in response to my other problems with my heart, leaves me gasping for air. I have come to deal with this by playing and replaying one section of Johannes Brahms' Ein Deutsches Requiem in my head. The section is taken from our liturgy and is entitled "How lovely are thy dwelling-places, O Lord of Hosts." If that section of music is done and I am still awake,

I switch to another section of the Requiem, and in seemingly no time I awake to the sound of my alarm.

How shall I then deal with the tumult and upset caused by the growing discord of my aging body? It rebels at my demands that it carry me yet another day. I try to rationalize my situation. I am approaching my 89th birthday, and I celebrate my unflagging independence. I drive my car to more than just visits to doctors' offices, and I am still planning programs that include critical introductions by me to operas and other music.

What, if anything, shall I fear? My beloved cat, Pepper, will be cared for, I am certain. The classes I attend will be one person smaller, but they will go on. The music programs I am running will be taken over by someone else or perhaps not. Each of us is just a small dot on the gigantic canvas of humanity. *For me, the presence of my daughters and grand-children is something I will miss. What new things will they be doing? Where are they? Are they happy?* I will miss them, but I will not miss the seemingly unstoppable pain of trying to exist.

I have lived a terrific 88 years, escaping Nazi Germany, being saved in the wonderful USA, marrying my Judy, and seeing my daughters mature and become successful mothers to their children. No one could want more.

Steve died on April 3, 2019.

Glossary of Terms

Administrator – A person appointed by a court to manage and dispose of the estate of a person who has left no will.

Adult Family Home – Private homes licensed by the state to provide individualized senior care and room and board to no more than six adults at a time.

Adult Protective Services/APS – Each state's agency focusing on the protection of seniors. The National Adult Protective Services Association (NAPSA) provides a map with links to local APS offices across the US. www.http//napsa-now.org/gethelp/help-in-your-area.

Advancement – Money that is loaned by a person to a prospective estate beneficiary, with the expectation that it will be repaid at death.

Affirmative Duty – The obligation to act.

Agent – A person chosen by a principal to act when the principal cannot act independently. Also referred to as an "attorney-in-fact."

Alzheimer's Disease – A type of dementia. It is an irreversible, progressive and eventually terminal disease, which, over time, erases memory, impairs information processing and judgment, and destroys the brain's ability to direct or perform the body's functions.

Burial Directive – A written document outlining each person's wishes regarding the disposition of final remains, burial and interment, as well as designating a surrogate to give these directions.

Capacity – The mental ability to understand one's actions and the consequences that flow from engaging in certain actions such as writing a will or a contract. To be capacitated means that you understand the nature of a transaction and are able to make voluntary and fully informed decisions. See ***Incapacitated***.

Care Manager – A professional, often a nurse or person with social work skills who is hired to assist a person or a family in developing a home-based plan of care that meets the senior's needs.

Care Plan – A written document that identifies nursing orders, protocols and specific health goals for a patient.

Dementia – A set of symptoms including memory loss, word-finding difficulties and poor judgment that affect the brain and mental processes.

Descent and Distribution – The plan set out in each state's laws for who will be entitled to inherit property from the estate of a person who dies and leaves no will.

Discharge Planner – An employee of a hospital or other treatment center who makes plans for ongoing care for patients who are going home and will require support.

Estate Planning – The process of designating who will be a fiduciary under powers of attorney, also the action of creating a written plan, properly witnessed and attested, for the disposition of assets at death.

Exploitation – Using resources belonging to another person without that person's knowledge or consent to gain financial benefit.

Fiduciary – Describing a person who stands in a trusted and confidential relationship to another.

Guardian *ad Litem* – A person appointed by a court in a legal proceeding to represent the interests of a minor (under age 18) or incapacitated person (subject to a guardianship).

Guardianship – A court-established process to provide ongoing management of the personal needs and/or property interests of a person who is deemed to be incapacitated.

Healthcare agent – A person designated to make healthcare decisions for another person during a period of incapacity. Sometimes called a "healthcare proxy" or a "healthcare surrogate."

Incapacitated – A term describing a person who, over time, has demonstrated an inability to provide adequately for his own shelter, hygiene, nutrition and finances.

Intestate – Dying without a will.

Living Will/Healthcare Directive – A written document ("advance directive") prepared by an attorney regarding the healthcare actions a person wishes to be taken after the attending physician certifies he or she is beyond hope of recovery.

NAELA – The National Academy of Elder Law Attorneys whose members focus their legal practices on estate planning and legal issues affecting seniors and their families. A directory of affiliated elder law attorneys is available at www.naela.org.

Non-Compliance – The condition of a person under a physician's care who fails to follow doctor's orders regarding prescription medicine and other treatments.

POLST/Physician Orders Regarding Life-Sustaining Treatments – Physician's orders concerning end-of-life medical treatments for a person experiencing such illness or frailty that the healthcare professional has determined that this person is not reasonably expected to live more than one year. www.polst.org/about-the-national-polst-paradigm/what-is-polst.

Power of Attorney – A document under which a principal grants authority to an agent to make decisions for and stand in the shoes of the principal. The power of attorney becomes effective as stated in the document and remains effective until revoked by the principal or by a court (if a guardianship is needed) or until the principal dies.

Principal – The individual who executes a power of attorney and designates an agent.

Probate – The legal process of "proving" a will and having it accepted by a court as the last testament of the deceased person. During the probate process, the personal representative ("executor") identifies all of the deceased person's property, locates the heirs, pays off any creditors, and distributes the deceased person's assets under the terms of the probated will.

Revocable Living Trust – A method for creating a plan during one's lifetime regarding the distribution of an estate at death that is outside the court system.

Self-neglect – The failure of a person to provide for his own basic needs of housing, nutrition, hygiene and medical care.

Skilled Nursing Facility – Provides continuous nursing care, room and board to people who require this level of medical attention and assistance in performing the required activities of daily living.

Springing Power of Attorney – A power of attorney that is activated ("springs into effect") upon the occurrence of a designated event, such as a doctor's certification of incapacity.

Stockholm Syndrome – A psychological phenomenon under which victims empathize and ally with the criminals who are hurting them.

Temporary Restraining Order/TRO – An order signed by a judge that imposes short-term restrictions on a third party's conduct (i.e. negating the third party's ability to contact or influence another party) prior to an actual court hearing.

Vulnerable Adult – A person over age 60 who has been deemed incapacitated by a court or who is receiving care services in his or her home, or in a residential setting.

Will – A written legal document that appoints someone to manage the estate and distribute his or her money and property at death.

www.ingramcontent.com/pod-product-compliance
Lightning Source LLC
Chambersburg PA
CBHW062008070426
42451CB00008BA/276